Ghost Stories from the Ghosts' Point of View Trilogy Vol. 1

Tina Erwin, CDR USN (Ret)

Ghost Stories from the Ghosts' Point of View, Trilogy
Vol. 1

Copyright © 2012 Tina Erwin

Third Edition Published 2022
Second Edition Published 2016
First Edition Published 2012

ISBN-13: 978-1-7322673-7-4

All rights reserved. No part of this book may be reproduced or transmitted in any form or by any means, electronic or mechanical, including photocopying, recording, or by any information storage and retrieval system, without permission in writing from the author at: **tinaerwin.com**

Cover Photography by Tina Erwin
Cover Location: Torc Falls,
Killarney, Ireland

Works by Tina Erwin

The Lightworker's Guide to Healing Grief

The Lightworker's Guide to Everyday Karma

Ghost Stories from the Ghosts' Point of View, Trilogy, Vol. 1

Ghost Stories from the Ghosts' Point of View, Trilogy, Vol. 2

Ghost Stories from the Ghosts' Point of View, Trilogy, Vol. 3

Soul Evolution, Past Lives and Karmic Ties

Karma and Frequency

The Crossing Over Prayer Book

Special Notice to the Reader:

WARNING
Due to the mature nature of the content of this book, which may deal with tragic and/or violent death, reader discretion is advised. These true stories are intended for mature audiences only.

Acknowledgments

Tremendous effort is required to put forth the information you are about to read, and no successful author accomplishes anything alone. I am blessed to have so many wonderful people supporting me as I share this critical knowledge of how the living can help the dead.

My loyal and loving husband has earned my undying gratitude for supporting all of my psychic efforts and for his conscientious editing work on these books.

I would like to gratefully acknowledge the support and critical assistance of my entire publishing team: my daughter, Jeanne Marie Erwin Coronado, my daughters–in-law Amee Erwin, and Monica Lane. A special thanks to my sister Andrea, and her daughter Marisa Harris for all the efforts to help the dead in all the locations we have visited over the years.

Thanks to all of your dedication, hard work and attention to detail, the world will get to know the true stories of those ghostly souls who will now live in our hearts forever.

Dedication

This entire book series is dedicated to all of my friends who, over the years, have taught me so much.

This dedication is also intended for all of those brave souls who asked for help in assisting many a ghostly soul to cross over.

And finally, I am deeply grateful for the Spiritual Beings who unfailingly assist us all to guide lost and lonely souls to the Heaven World.

Preface

Sometimes when you have some modest level of psychic ability, you are blessed when you can use this skill in the service of others. Some psychics talk to the dead. Some tell futures, some predict dire events, and some help the police department.

In my case, I discovered almost twenty years ago that I could actually see ghosts and assist them to cross over. At first, I did not fully realize how critical this assistance would become for those who have died difficult deaths. What kind of death would that be?

A difficult death is one where the soul may have died by suicide, been murdered, died in battle or in an emotional place where the soul feels that somehow, something about themselves is not worthy of God's love. The energy of these souls, these ancestors of time gone by, impacts those of us living today.

In my studies of Feng Shui, I became aware of predecessor energy, the energy of people who have lived on a spot of earth many centuries before the current owners. I came to realize how powerful negative predecessor energy is in the manner in which it can tragically impact the current owners. Out of this understanding, I realized that usually, when a ghost 'haunts' a location, he, or she or even a group of souls usually is not doing it to harass the current owners. The ghost is either there existing 'psychically' in the time in which they used to live, or the person has no idea that he or she has actually died. On rare occasions the soul does realize that death has come for them, and he or she can still see mortal people in the current time.

Frankly, the more I studied the ghostly personages of the past, the more I realized what tremendous theme and variation exists in their reasons for not crossing over into the Heaven World. However, what they all had in common was a reason that crossing over seemed impossible for each of them. They needed help in their spiritual process because their method of death or their negative feelings about themselves at death made transition seem impossible. I also realized that if any psychic can see or hear a ghost, that soul has very probably not crossed over into the light. I became chillingly aware that simply having a conversation with a ghost was not helpful to the soul. Ghosts truly need help from the living.

Over the years while assisting thousands of souls to make that transition into the light of the Heaven World, I heard their stories. Some were of judgment gone terribly wrong, some of horrific murders, and some were of towering guilt and self-hatred. As I shared these stories with family and friends, each person told me that this perspective, this ghost's perspective, was unique, something that he or she would never have previously considered.

So, at the urging of friends and family, I present to

you Ghost Stories from the Ghosts' Point of View. Each story you are about to read explains what has happened to a particularly memorable person who has died, and why he or she did not cross over into the light. More stories/books will follow because I have volumes of these stories.

Meet them, hear them and then I am asking you to open your hearts to each of their situations.

However, I do have to warn you that the reason that predecessor energy is so powerful is that the ghost's experience is usually one of tremendous emotion and that dynamic energy is why you are feeling that ghost's presence. Therefore, listening to and reading about their experiences may challenge you, unnerve you and hopefully move you as much as they have moved me.

I encourage you to read these stories with an open mind and a compassionate heart. Think about it: the help that each of these souls is requesting could be the very need that each of us would want to receive if we were trapped as a ghost in another time and place.

Sometimes, it will take courage to read these true stories. I hope that after you meet these souls, you will never feel the same again about a ghost. Perhaps you will no longer be fearful of them but will say The Crossing Over Prayer included at the end of this book. This service of helping the dead is the truest essence of doing light work and ultimately will be the compassion that you will want for yourself.

Tina Erwin

Foreword

Tina has had many firsthand experiences with ghosts, and she has helped thousands of souls to cross over into Heaven. Many years ago, Tina explained to my family and me, that ghosts need help and that we don't need to be afraid of them. Throughout the years, she has taught us how to help them and to realize that they have the same basic needs that every living person has, including the need for comfort and love. They also have the same personality in death as they had while they were alive. I have come to realize, that for a ghost to exist, a human being (or an animal) had to have been born, live some length of time and then die.

However, what may surprise you is that not everyone moves directly into the light. There are many reasons for this. Some souls do not understand that they are dead, some are angry or guilty, and some linger, at times creating problems for the living. Each person, each soul has a story about their life and their death. Some causes of death are surprising, some terrifying, and others so poignant that they will break your heart. I learned that their personalities are still there, their fears are just as powerful, and their desire to have someone hear them, is a constant challenge.

I have heard many an individual say: "I have a ghost in my house, and I want to keep them here because it is such a curiosity." These ghosts are not a curiosity. These are real people in a different dimension that need help to cross over. Yes, ghost stories can be scary, but it can be scary for the ghosts too. My sister, Tina, has been able to show us another view - the ghosts' view. After you 'experience' this book, I can guarantee that you will never think about ghosts the same way.

What makes these stories so much more powerful is that they are all true. All ghost stories are about real people who had difficult deaths, or who may have had unresolved emotional problems or severe traumas. I hope you will join me in opening your heart to souls on the other side now that you are finally able to hear their real-life stories from their point of view.

Andrea Harris

Mission Statement

The purpose of this book is to offer you a different view of what it is like to leave your body at death.

The hope of this book is that you will cease your fear of souls who have left their physical bodies and begin to understand their situation.

The opportunity of this book is the opening of your compassionate heart to those who need help crossing over.

Send them your prayers.

Send these souls your love.

Request Angels of Transition as you say The Crossing Over Prayer to assist them in crossing into the light, no matter their method of death, no matter what this person may have been like in life, and no matter whether or not you loved them or even knew them. You can find more prayers to help the living and the dead in The Crossing Over Prayer Book©

Service to the dead is one of the most compassionate and important acts of kindness, a living person can ever do. <u>No ghost is at peace until he or she finally crosses over into the light.</u> Your service to them means the difference between continual feelings of fear and abandonment, cold and pain versus the joy, and the hopeful delight of crossing into heaven.

Table of Contents

An Introduction to the World of Ghosts _____1
The House on Botany Bay Boulevard _____7
Annabelle _____25
The Rocket Scientist _____35
The Adorable Red Mazda _____47
The Brake Signal _____53
Absolute Control _____59
Their Accusing Eyes _____69
The Intruder _____81
The House of the Underground Railroad _____93
Terror in 1939 _____101
Bertha Sue _____111
Such an Incredible Stench _____121
Her Punishment _____131
The Exit Strategy _____143
Helen Stanton _____153
On the Wagon Train _____165
The Tennessee Property _____173

Her Sorrowful Heart	185
The Dallas Cowboys	193
The Oneida Shaman	203
The Witness Protection Program	215
Explaining the Physics of Metaphysics	225
My Own Spiritual Service	231
Prayers for Sending Ghosts to the Heaven World	237
Glossary	251
About the Author	265

An Introduction to the World of Ghosts

Being of Service to the Dead

If you, gentle reader, do not take anything else from these stories, perhaps you will come to understand the sheer volume of predecessor energy and ghosts that are out there. The ghosts' stories you are about to read are all true. There are thousands more. There are thousands more haunted households out there seeking help and believing that no one will believe them when they say that their home is haunted. I lived through that. I know how it feels to live in one of those toxic homes. Please read about my experience in the story The House on Botany Bay Boulevard. Most of us never think about these things, but they are there, nonetheless.

Every house has a story. The older the home, the more complicated its history. Even new homes may have the influence of predecessor energy, the events of previous people who lived on that spot of Earth.

Natural events that have happened on a spot of land centuries ago can influence those living there today. There are few perfect spots on Earth. There are no perfect houses. Levels of negativity exist to greater or lesser degrees in everyone's home or office building. The happier and healthier the owners are, the more positive their home will be.

The truth is that people do not start out their lives thinking that they are going to be divorced, lose a child, have a fire, or suffer a terrible financial catastrophe. However, in the experiential laboratory that is mortal life, things, sometimes, tragic things happen to people. The energy of these events lives in the homes in which they dwell. Even people who do not consider themselves sensitive can feel it.

True Spiritual Service: The Essence of Light Work

Those conscientious souls on a spiritual path understand that we are all here for service. The more this concept lives within you, the more you will find that your life is only about service to the Earth, to animals and to people. But there is so much more that true Lightworkers can do.

The information you are about to read will now take you to a much higher level of service and that is service to the dead. Service to the dead is of critical importance. The more you can cease your fear of ghosts, the more you can realize that your help and your compassion for their plight will be the very help and compassion that you will seek at your own death. You will be living the pure essence of karmic law: what you will do for someone else may be the service

An Introduction to the World of Ghosts

that someone will do for you. You cannot know the spiritual importance of this service.

When approached with a sincere heart, great spiritual service can be provided to lost, cold, confused, and desperate souls on the other side who need your help. Imagine for a moment what it is like to be dead:

- No one can see you.
- No one can hear you.
- No one warned you about this.
- You may or may not see other souls.
- The world around you is chronically gray.
- A profound loneliness permeates your soul.
- There may be scary things that come at you.
- There is no one recognizable to ask for help.
- You miss how food tastes. You miss the physical senses.
- You are leaderless in a barren land where neither time, space nor gravity exist.
- If you died a violent death, you may see your butchered body for a brief time and then suddenly you stop seeing it.
- You are wandering around in what is called the 'astral plane,' that 4th dimensional place between the mortal 3rd dimensional world and the 5th dimensional Heaven World.
- You may not even realize that you are dead. You can still see your body, but oddly, you never change your clothes. You are wearing the clothes – or lack of clothes – in which you died until you are able to cross over.
- You travel at the speed of thought. You can find yourself instantly in front of any relative who crosses

Ghost Stories from the Ghosts' Point of View

your mind.
- You may or may not see the Light of Transition. When or if it comes for you, you may have no idea that you should go toward it.
- You are not actually able to 'walk.' You cannot feel that comforting grounding that gravity provides for you. We take gravity and time for granted. In the astral, in the 4th dimension, they do not exist.
- You cannot see your feet, because there is no gravity with which to ground you in any physical reality. It also explains why you can travel with the speed of thought.
- And you feel so cold! The cold penetrates you, especially if you drowned. One of the most profound effects of death and landing in the lower astral is the feeling of cold, of hunger, of being dirty, of never finding comfort. That denial of comfort is so important to understand, because even though you no longer have a physical body, the physical sensations of heat and cold, hunger and feeling dirty continue in the psyche of the soul. These sensations persist until the soul crosses into the Heaven World.

Imagine how terrifying it would be to wander a world without understanding what has happened to you.

Imagine how astounded you would be to find someone who was willing to swallow his or her own fear and want to help you.

Imagine your gratitude at receiving assistance in making that transition to the Heaven World. Imagine how many prayers you would send to the kind soul who helped you to cross over.

Imagine how grateful you would be to understand

that the Light of Transition could be for you and that stepping into that light was the right thing to do.

Imagine.

Remote Viewing

Many psychics or mediums physically visit a location to determine if it is haunted. This isn't entirely necessary. Many people use a practice called remote viewing (also called psychic vision) to scan a location once the owner has given permission. It is a very efficient way to handle any property and any ghost who might be haunting a location. This method can also provide a bit better protection for the psychic than physically visiting a haunted location.

Some remote viewers see in real time, meaning he or she can see current furniture, colors, and situations. Other remote viewers see through stacks of time and examine what occurred in that location in the past. Occasionally the overlay of real time is visible for them, but mostly, they see into what is called the 'ether' or 4th dimension realm. This is the realm of ghosts. This is where the real work takes place.

Angelic Service

Angels of Transition are absolutely instrumental in assisting lost and confused souls to cross over. Their patience, kindness and compassion are always available to all of us. We have only to ask for their help for ourselves or a deceased loved one.

I have always marveled at the work of the angels who have joined me in assisting the many ghosts who have made this transition. I always find myself feeling

Ghost Stories from the Ghosts' Point of View

a deep and profound gratitude for their service to all of the unique personalities that they so patiently and lovingly escort to the other side.

The House on Botany Bay Boulevard

My husband and I spent over twenty years in the Navy. We were always stationed where there was a submarine presence because we both worked for the Submarine Force. In June of 1979, my husband and I were both Lieutenants in the Navy and we were returning from a tour in Naples, Italy. We received orders to Charleston, South Carolina, where my husband would become the navigator on a ballistic missile submarine. My new job was also working for a submarine command in Charleston. I was pregnant with our oldest son James and finding a home in the sticky summer heat of Charleston was exhausting. We looked at dozens of houses. Some homes I just knew when I walked in that they were haunted. Others, I was not too sure. We did finally find a house . . . and what a house! I did not feel that it was haunted when we bought it. Maybe it was not haunted at closing. However, things were about to change in that house.

Here is the paranormal story of our seven years in Charleston.

The Archdale Plantation

Who knew that our first home would be in the haunted neighborhood of the Archdale Plantation in Charleston, South Carolina? The house was a mere 18 months old in 1979, but from the moment I moved in, I knew it was haunted. My husband was away in Navigator school in Virginia, so I moved in by myself, with just a few things to get by. I had to wait a month for our household goods to arrive from Italy, so I camped out in the house.

An empty house echoes, even a carpeted house echoes and I found myself feeling slightly uncomfortable, besides being pregnant in the Charleston heat. I felt so alone in that 2500 square foot house. I didn't know anyone in the neighborhood and there is so much to do when you move. I was exhausted each night when I went to bed. But I could have gotten past the fatigue and the newness had the eerie sounds not begun the very first night I spent in that empty, exceptionally quiet house. I remember turning out the light and trying to fall asleep on my air mattress. I knew I had to adjust to the sounds of a new house, but I was not expecting to hear human sounds, the sound of someone walking in the rafters above my head.

I could distinctly hear heavy footfalls walking directly above my bedroom. I remember lying there terrified in that big house. I became aware that I was holding my breath as I was listening. When you realize that you are not alone in an empty 'echoy'

The House on Botany Bay Boulevard

house, at first you think that it must be an intruder. But you know that you have been through the whole house, and you know for sure, that no one is physically there. Your mind races through the slim possibilities of what could create this sound. I knew that eventually I have to go up into the attic and investigate this odd noise. I found myself so afraid that I couldn't get up to search it out. The tension of fear that tightened every muscle of my body was exhausting. I was flooded with adrenaline as my mind raced through the 'what ifs'.

What if the footsteps leave the attic?

What if the footsteps come down the stairs from the attic and start toward my bedroom?

What if this is a real person who got in somehow? But if this is a ghost, oh my God, what if I come face to face with this ghost? What do I do then? What if he wishes me harm? Can he harm me? How do you remove a ghost?

I felt utterly alone with this sleep-robbing problem. It was a very long night. Finally, the footfalls stopped, and I guess I fell asleep. The next morning, I climbed all over the rafter area, but there was no evidence that there was anyone or anything there. I knew it couldn't be an animal because these were decidedly human footfall noises, a man's footsteps to be exact.

Who do you tell about this? People who think they hear ghosts are often ridiculed. I was a Lieutenant in the Navy for heaven's sake. These things aren't something a Naval Officer would routinely talk about, so I just didn't mention it.

Pretty soon, though, there were new phenomena: pounding on the walls, or knocking, sometimes above my head. I wanted to ignore it all, but I realized that this ghost would not be ignored.

Predecessor Energy

I was baffled about how an 18-month-old house could possibly be haunted. I did not know there is something called 'predecessor energy,' the energy of the people who have previously lived on the land. The previous energies of the events that had taken place in the past were haunting me. What I didn't understand at the time is that for the souls stuck in that time, well, there is no time. There is only the eternal moment of the dimension in which they are living. It doesn't matter how many new structures are placed in a spot, the energy of the past, of the souls who are or who were present as ghosts, still exists. That energy doesn't just 'go away' when you tear the house down or people move. It is such a strange concept to embrace, but it is true globally.

Millions of people have lived and died on the Earth. Some of them violently, through the traumas of wars, earthquakes, hurricanes, murders, fires, floods. Violent/traumatic death can cause souls to remain in a location for hundreds of years, waiting for --- something. They don't know that they are waiting for something, but nothing changes for them and oddly, they do not notice this. Time has no meaning for them. They don't notice that they never change the clothes they wore at their death. Yet, the animation of who that soul was in mortal life remains; the soul's personality is constant and is active. Their emotions are also still active, meaning that soul can be just as enraged in death as he or she was in life. Conversely

The House on Botany Bay Boulevard

the soul can be just as kindly and loving as well.

All ghosts operate in the 4th dimension. If you can see, hear, or sense a ghost, or if a psychic can talk to a ghost, then this means that this soul has not transitioned to the Heaven World. However, as a pregnant Lieutenant in the Navy in 1979, I didn't know any of this. All I knew was that we purchased a haunted house. I had no idea what more would come.

We Named Him Jake

We named him Jake and he was a thief. He stole my son's tennis shoes, a bottle of wine, a diamond from one of earrings and three contact lenses from my husband's contact lens case. My wallet disappeared during the night as well as postcards, letters, and gold bracelets. It is unnerving to realize that you put an object down, closed your eyes, went to sleep, and then awaken to find that this object has vanished. Who wants to believe that a ghost is taking your things? We could not fathom this, so we took the house apart over and over searching for these things that were never, ever found, even after we moved.

But Jake had more in store for us than just petty theft.

One cold, terrifying morning we awoke to find every single window and door open – and the whole house alarm was still set! I remember standing there, looking at this evidence of the paranormal, while the hair stood up on my whole body and a cold chill swept down my spine.

How can a ghost do this, Troy and I screamed at each other. Was this an evil ghost? Was this some Charleston devil, who had come to live at our house?

Ghost Stories from the Ghosts' Point of View

What kind of a paranormal power is this? What kind of a power does this ghost have to be able to manipulate matter like this? How can he make things disappear, override alarm systems, and move objects like doors and windows and never make a sound? Can fear become chronic? I pondered this because I found myself constantly looking over my shoulder, not trusting my senses and waiting for something unnatural and terrible to happen to me, to us.

Sometimes it sounded like he was washing dishes in the kitchen. He so terrified our Siamese cats that when Jake was the most active, they would stick to me like glue. I never knew what he did to the cats, but they could see him, so I knew he was not my imagination. Animals can see in the 4th dimension, so animals can see ghosts. However, this was no comfort at the time.

Jake became far more brazen as time went on. I supposed to him, tormenting us was sport. Of course, the problem was, this was not fun for us. We had to decide if we could handle the banging on the walls, the petty theft, and the noises. We discussed moving but it would be at our own expense, and we could not afford it at the time and so far, Jake had not been horrible, just mischievous. Really, how would we explain that we had to move from a house that we just bought? What if we couldn't sell the house? The logistics of this were too overwhelming.

The Unimaginable Happens

So, we settled into our haunted house life. It's funny how you force yourself to adjust to something that you can't fully explain, and you cannot share.

The House on Botany Bay Boulevard

However, there are those things that unnerve you to your core and cause you to question whether or not you are learning to live with a ghost.

One night when my husband was at home and not at sea, we finished our day, put sweet baby James to bed and then turned in ourselves. It was quiet in the Charleston countryside except for the drone of the air conditioners. I suppose, with Troy home from sea, for a while, we rather forgot about Jake. He had become part of the landscape of our lives, and we had learned to ignore the things he was doing . . . until that night. Obviously, he did not want to be ignored.

This night will live for me as one ghastly unforgettable moment. I'm sure I was in a deep sleep and yet when it happened, I was electrified with fear. All the hair on my body was standing up. I think the fact that I could feel my terror pulled me out of the sleep state. It is one thing when the ghost makes noise, bangs on walls and is generally just a nuisance. It is a whole new ballgame when the ghost takes his intimidation to an extremely intimate level.

He wanted it to seem sexual, terrifying, and powerful. I didn't have to be psychic to feel his intentions.

Very deliberately, very slowly, he lay down beside me. I remember distinctly being able to feel his entire icy body positioned close to mine.

Time stood still.

I could not breathe.

I could feel him, but I could not see him.

A type of paralysis took over and I became a prisoner in a body that could not move, could not breathe, and could not cry out. A silent scream formed in my mind, but I could not get my throat or my mouth to work. My husband was inches from me, and I could call out to him.

This was not a dream. I was wide-awake, with the gnawing awareness that I had no power to stop him from doing anything he wanted to do to me.

. . . . And then he came even closer.

When he slipped his hand into mine, I thought death would come to me and that I was destined to join his ghostly existence. My accelerating heart felt as if it would burst from my chest. I had never known such powerlessness in the waking state. Is this what a woman feels like just before she is about to be raped?

My husband was lying on the other side of me, and I could not speak to tell him that I was being touched by the hand of death. I was motionless and at the same time my mind was screaming for help. The interminable seconds ticked by in an agony of slow motion as I waited for what was to happen next. Breathe, I reminded myself. Nauseating questions pummeled my thoughts.

What is he planning to do next?

How can I feel the body of a ghost beside me?

How do you describe the indescribable?

How am I able to feel his long, boney, icy fingers?

Was handholding just a sickening prelude to something far more sexual?

He must have decided that he had tortured me long enough, because in an agony of slow-motion action, he withdrew his hand from mine. I felt that this one action must have taken twenty minutes. I had no idea that letting go of someone's hand could take such an excruciatingly long time.

The House on Botany Bay Boulevard

Then I felt him move his body away from mine. And I knew with a sickening certainty that even though he was not in bed with me any longer, he was still in the room, watching me, watching us. What kind of a sick soul was this man, this ghost? It was at that moment, that I became frantic to figure out how to rid our lives of this terrifying presence.

Little did I realize how much more there was to come . . .

How do you get rid of a ghost this sinister, this diabolical and this powerful?

So Much More to Come

During this time, my sister was living with us while she went to college in Charleston... and she heard him too. Sometimes she and I were so freaked out that we would at first question each other about the things that Jake was doing. A prime example was awakening to finding all the doors open in the winter (and it does get quite cold in Charleston.) This was a totally different event from the previous episode of awakening to find all the windows and doors being open. We just stared at each other. Was Jake showing off? Was he trying to terrify both of us?

One morning our alarm clocks did not go off. Yet, it seemed as if Jake was watching out for us and pounded on the wall above my husband's head. This was the first time my husband had experienced Jake's intervention into our lives. We quickly got up and left for work. I realized that 90% of all of the incidents happened when Troy was at sea. Jake seldom 'visited' us when Troy was at home except of course for that one terrifying night visit. Maybe Jake

Ghost Stories from the Ghosts' Point of View

felt we (my sister, baby James, and I) didn't need his ghostly help when Troy was home.

One morning, my Datsun 810 station wagon refused to start as I was leaving for work. I couldn't figure out what was wrong with the car, so I drove my husband's 240Z to work (because Troy was at sea.) When I returned home, I had the Datsun towed to my mechanic's shop in Summerville. The mechanic got the car off the tow truck, and it started right up. I was dumbfounded. However, my Datsun expert went over the car and discovered that there was a dangerous issue in the engine. Apparently, driving that car would have definitely resulted in an accident. Here again, another chill went down my spine. I was grateful to have been spared. Was this Jake looking out for me?

Who was this bizarre ghost? Certain times he terrified us, other times he seemed to play games with us and then he would be helpful and protective of all of us. What a paradox. I guess I thought that ghosts were either good or bad, but this guy was all over the map as the encounters continued.

One evening we were all together in our den talking. Everyone was present including both Siamese and my husband when it happened: someone with heavy footsteps ran down the hall. It's those moments when you catch your breath, stare at each other, profoundly grateful that you had a witness to what you unmistakably heard. No, you didn't imagine this. Someone or something just ran down the hall and there is no one there. This so unnerved us that my ever-the-engineering-minded husband decided to set up a video camera to see if we could catch him on tape. We taped that hallway for hours, but he either

The House on Botany Bay Boulevard

didn't appear, or just didn't run down the hall during the filming. We had four hours of video snow and no Jake.

My husband was reading to our two-year old son one evening, when they both heard a giant hand pound the outside of our house. It was so powerful they could hear plaster residue falling inside the wall. We heard those wall poundings often.

One night, after we had a party, someone left us a bottle of Mateus Rose wine. I remember placing it on a counter. My sister remembered seeing it. The next morning, the wine was gone. We never found it. Jake was at it again. My sister asked me if ghosts were able to drink wine. I told her I had no idea. The ever-changing dimension to this ghost baffled us – and still the events continued.

One Halloween night we had a party and, though I know it sounds cliché, something supernatural happened. After all of our friends left, we cleaned up, then my sister and I sat on my bed to chat about the party. My husband was at sea. The Siamese were sitting beside us when we all heard what sounded like several people in our kitchen doing dishes. Think about this: our house was super quiet; baby James was asleep, and you could literally hear a pin drop in that house. Then we begin to hear the unmistakable – and unnatural – sounds of clanking dishes, clinking glasses, and colliding pots and pans. The look in the giant blue eyes of the Siamese was pure fear. The happy atmosphere in the house had become chilled to the point that we could all feel our skin crawl. The cats knew that sound was not natural. Their fur began to stand up on both of their chocolate bodies and they looked like the traditional scary Halloween cats: all puffed up, backs arched and hissing. They looked all around expecting to see something coming to harm them. I'm not sure what caused my sister and me more abject fear: the cats or the sounds. But the evening was obviously younger than we thought because more was to come.

As we were listening, the kitchen sounds ceased, and we heard what we thought was someone trying to break into the house. We didn't understand. Was this Jake playing more games? She and I (and the cats) were so terrified we felt rooted to my bed. But we realized that if someone really was trying to break in, we had to do something.

My sister called her boyfriend and then we called the police. The police and my sister's boyfriend arrived at the same time and together they inspected the house. I remember how terrified I was to have to turn off the alarm system to be able to let the police in when they arrived. To turn off the alarm system, meant that I had to walk down the hall near that kitchen. I have never been so relieved to see a police officer in my life.

The police believed that our call to them and their arrival had scared away someone trying to break into the house. What baffled the police was that there was no way we could have heard that noise from the bedroom. It was only the crazy noise of someone doing dishes and other unnerving noises that caused us to call the police. The police discovered scratch marks on the back door of the house as if someone was trying to jimmy the lock. Our call and the arrival of the police must have scared him off. Did Jake protect

The House on Botany Bay Boulevard

us while Troy was gone?

We Discover We're Not Alone with Our Plight

I did believe that Jake needed to move on, to cross over. But how could I get him to do that? My frustration with this house was so great that I contacted the Duke University Department for Paranormal studies. They were of no help. They only studied ghosts; they didn't know how to help a ghost cross over.

I decided that I must not be the only one with this problem, so I then began to study how to remove ghosts. But at the time I could not find much written on this topic.

I tried simple prayers.

I asked the ghost to leave.

I quickly discovered that burning sage was worthless.

I felt like Jake was laughing at me. Despite all of my efforts, nothing I tried got him to depart our house. I simply had no practical experience in removing a stubbornly entrenched, extremely active ghost.

About this time, my sister, Andrea decided to do research into this neighborhood to see if there was any history written about this area. We were greatly relieved to learn what she discovered.

All of the homes in the neighborhood were about 2-4 years old. However, the land had a rich, fascinating history. The Archdale Plantation was built by Richard Baker, with a land grant of 300 acres from King Charles on April 1, 1681, as the Archdale Plantation along the Ashley River in South Carolina.

Ghost Stories from the Ghosts' Point of View

Historians believe that the plantation may have been named after Sarah Archdale Baker, who was the mother of the first Richard Baker to immigrate to South Carolina from the island of Barbados. Imagine how many generations of people had lived and died on the over 3000 acres that eventually comprised this property. The plantation grew indigo and rice. There were family members, friends and relatives who would have enjoyed this beautiful land. There were also slaves who worked this plantation. My sister and I had long speculated on who Jake had been in that life. She felt he was a slave. I thought he was a foreman, not a slave. Perhaps we will never know.

This was my first introduction to predecessor energy: the energy of the previous people who had lived on a property. The sad part of this was that the Archdale plantation house itself actually survived the ravages of the Civil war, only to be destroyed by a 7.3 earthquake on August 31, 1886, where one hundred people died. This meant that the house and the neighborhood were also on a fault line. The energy of a fault line will facilitate the presence of a ghost simply because of the unstable nature of fault line energy. At the time, however, I didn't know any of this.

In desperation, my sister and I reluctantly plucked up our courage, and spoke to my neighbors about the ghostly activity we were experiencing. We were relieved to discover that they, too, had their own ghost stories to tell:

One neighbor came down each morning to find all of her furniture completely rearranged. Now mind you, she never heard a sound. How do you rearrange an entire room of furniture silently? This so unhinged her,

The House on Botany Bay Boulevard

that she moved.

Another couple heard horses clomping all night long. They told us they believed that their home was built where a stable once stood. Were these ghost horses? Can animals be ghosts too?

One lady came downstairs each morning to the scene of a rocking chair gently rocking. The chair had been physically moved in front of a now blank wall. Obviously, a long time ago, there had probably been a window in that exact location.

Our next-door neighbor also had jewelry stolen. But her jewelry was eventually returned. Nothing Jake stole from us was ever found or returned, even when we moved from Charleston. This neighbor also told us that she walked into her bathroom one morning to find every single surface covered in water droplets. Not puddles, but individual droplets that uniformly covered the counters, toilet seat and floors. Nothing in her bathroom leaked and her ceiling was dry. She said she and her husband also heard footsteps throughout the house and there was no one there.

Some homeowners told us they saw ghostly apparitions in their bedrooms at night. That so unnerved my sister, that when she when to sleep, she turned out the light and put the covers over her head. She absolutely did not want to see Jake or any ghostly apparitions!

The stories were endless. We realized we were not crazy, and we were not alone.

Finally, six years and two kids later, my husband and I, now both Lieutenant Commanders in the Navy, were given orders to Norfolk, Virginia. At last, we could leave our haunted house! But first, we had to sell this property.

We never told our real estate agent that the home was haunted. We were not sure she would believe us. However, she must have figured it out because in the summer of 1985, in the oppressive, humid, Charleston heat, she refused to stay in the house during all of the many open houses she hosted. She sat on the front steps and showed people inside and then she waited outside on those steps. When I asked her why, all she would say was that the house gave her the creeps.

It took us seven long months to sell that house. We then discovered that the new owners spent one night in the house and turned around the next day and put it back on the market. Obviously, they didn't like the welcome Jake must have prepared for them.

Within a year of the sale of our Charleston home, the State of South Carolina passed a law that required a homeowner to disclose that a residence was haunted. I found it interesting that you had to disclose that it was haunted, not just that someone had died there within five years, which is the law in many states, including California. That made sense because South Carolina has had deaths from the Revolutionary War, the Civil War and the many slave related deaths that occurred in that area. Obviously, the state of South Carolina believes in ghosts: maybe it's time for the rest of us to jump on that logic bandwagon. We were glad to leave Charleston.

Blessedly, the house we purchased in Virginia Beach in Witch Duck Point did not appear to be haunted. However, I often asked myself if my life could get any weirder. Witch Duck Point was thusly named because it was here, in the 1700s that women accused of witchcraft were ducked or drowned. However, no witches ever haunted us in our house there. We had three peaceful ghost free years before we were transferred to California.

Epilogue

I have spent the last thirty years learning how to clear property, how to assist ghosts in moving on, and how to make sense out of paranormal activity. Maybe Jake was my introduction into a life of service to the dead. Unfortunately, in a final irony, if Jake is still in the house on Botany Bay, I cannot help him. Along the way, I learned about Spiritual Law, meaning that you have to have a homeowner's permission to remove a ghost. Since we no longer own that house, I do not have permission to assist him. However, because of him, I studied and learned how to help souls like him. Perhaps he will eventually find the light and make his way to the Heaven World. He was truly the one ghost I wish I could have 'spoken' to about who he was and his life, but alas, that was not to be.

The House on Botany Bay Boulevard

Annabelle

I never know how someone will find the help that he or she needs to remove a needy ghost. I am always privileged to be of service to those who find me, so one evening, when a lovely lady named Peggy, called me I was delighted to help.

Peggy was – in her words – 'desperate' to figure out what was psychically happening in her house. She told me that she had been searching for help for easily 18 months and not one psychic seemed to have an answer to her perplexing situation which centered on her eight-year-old daughter, Jocelyn.

Sometimes parents don't know what to believe when their children tell them things. What if your child sees something and you as the parent can't see it and you have no idea if what your child is telling you is true or not? How does a parent discern truth from fantasy? What is a parent to do when their son or daughter tells them that they are seeing a ghost? Some ghosts are benign, but Jocelyn's ghost was not friendly, and Peggy's daughter was growing more terrified with each passing day. Imagine if this were your situation, what would you do?

Ghost Stories from the Ghosts' Point of View

Night of Terror

Her piercing screams woke the whole family out of a sound sleep one cool San Diego night. Peggy and her husband ran to their eight-year-old daughter Jocelyn's room only to discover that she had fled her room in stark terror. The front door was wide open and there was their daughter tearing bare footed out of the house, dashing across the yard headed down the street.

Peggy's husband, Charles ran after their daughter, scooped her up and brought her back into the house where their other two daughters joined them. Jocelyn was crying and shaking. Her parents naturally assumed that she had had an extremely bad dream. What else could cause a child to react so violently in the middle of the night?

But Jocelyn assured them that this was no dream. She knew she was awake. She told them that she was sound asleep when she realized that someone was standing by her bed. She immediately opened her eyes to a terrifying sight: a little blonde girl about seven years old standing over her with a huge butcher knife threatening to kill her!

At first Peggy and her husband tried to reassure Jocelyn that this was just a bad dream. But Jocelyn was adamant this was no dream; there was a little girl in the house with a butcher knife. The problem was that no one could see this little girl but Jocelyn.

Her parents did their best to check out her room and assured her that whatever or whoever had been there, was gone now. The family tried to return to sleep. But Peggy was haunted by what her daughter had said. Jocelyn had always been a truthful child.

Where did she get this idea that there was another child in the house? What caused Peggy the most concern was that Jocelyn was adamant that she had not had a 'bad dream.' This was real to her. Little did Peggy know that things were about to escalate into a daily psychic drama.

The following morning, Jocelyn was more adamant than ever that this little girl had been there, so Peggy asked her what the child's name was. Jocelyn started to think about that answer when the little girl 'appeared' to her daughter again. Jocelyn became immediately excited and said that she could see her in the corner. Apparently, this child's name was Annabelle. Jocelyn was bewildered when her mom said that she didn't see anything in the corner. Jocelyn was insistent that there was a child in pink pajamas standing in the corner of their dining room. Great, Peggy thought, now I have three kids and a ghost child.

Annabelle's Rage

Annabelle was a viciously angry child and Jocelyn had no idea why. It was as if one day there were no ghosts in their house and then the next day this Annabelle ghost-child appeared. Where had she come from? Why was she there? Where was her family?

Peggy had no idea what to do with Annabelle. She couldn't see the child, but Jocelyn kept talking about her. As days turned to weeks and weeks turned to months, this ghost child haunted Jocelyn day and night. The butcher knife episodes continued. It was as if as time went on, this little ghost became angrier and angrier. How could this be? Night after night was punctuated with Jocelyn's screams, with her fear of sleeping alone in her room and with the demands from Jocelyn that Peggy "do something about this ghost."

While Peggy was trying to figure out the situation, Annabelle would take fiendish delight in terrifying their rabbit, Kenny. Their little adorable, (completely house trained) harmless rabbit lived in the house at night. Jocelyn said that some nights Annabelle would threaten to murder the rabbit with the butcher knife. Peggy began to realize that Jocelyn had to be telling the truth because the nights that Annabelle was terrorizing the rabbit, poor little Kenny would utter these odd throaty, rumbling sounds. These were rabbit sounds of great distress. It was as if he was being murdered. Peggy had never heard a rabbit make these utterances before. She didn't know rabbits could make any sound at all: they don't have vocal cords. Apparently, however, when a rabbit is profoundly terrified, it can emit a sound. The poor creature would also 'thump' his back leg like mad and on wood floors it echoed throughout the house.

Peggy noticed that the cat seemed to be able to see Annabelle as well. Sometimes she would also howl. Peggy began to wonder if anyone would ever be able to have another restful night's sleep again. She began to search for someone who could help her with this ghost situation. But where to do you find someone who can help you remove a ghost? There are all kinds of psychics on the Internet, but how do you determine who is legitimate?

All the psychics she spoke with told her that if she

Annabelle

burned sage, that the ghost would leave. Peggy burned so much sage that her smoke detector went off as the house filled with clouds of 'sagey' smelling smoke. Jocelyn said that defiant Annabelle just stood and watched: the sage was worthless and had no effect on her whatsoever. Peggy told Jocelyn to ask Annabelle why she was here.

Apparently, Annabelle wanted to join the family and she wanted Peggy to be her mom. Sometimes she would hug Peggy's legs hoping Peggy could feel her and would love her. Peggy also realized that getting Jocelyn to ask Annabelle to leave wouldn't work. Peggy had an emotional conundrum: on one hand her heart went out to this child and on the other hand she had to get such a terrifying figure out of her house.

When Peggy heard that Annabelle wanted her to be her mommy, she suddenly realized that Annabelle must have wanted to get rid of Jocelyn so that she, Peggy would now be her mom. What a chilling thought. Peggy wondered what had happened to Annabelle's mom. Why hadn't Annabelle crossed over? Don't all kids go to heaven right away when they die? How did this ghost child pick her house? Why? Was it that she was looking for a family? How long had she been dead? Where did she die? How did she pick Peggy's family? As Peggy was pondering these seemingly unanswerable questions, a chill ran down her spine. Was there something about her house or her family that made her attractive to this ghost and would more be coming? She also realized that her psychic eight-year-old daughter didn't have any answers to these questions either.

Peggy persisted in searching for a psychic who could remove Annabelle. However, she realized that she also needed to find someone who could help her with her now exceptionally psychic child, Jocelyn. What does a parent do with a psychic child who would appear to be magnetic to ghosts? Why were these ghosts attracted to her child? She learned through her own research that there were few books on this topic, lots of ghost stories, but no information on how to remove them.

The Heart of Compassion

I never fail to be astonished at how people find the right person to help them. In this case I had dinner with a friend who introduced me to a woman I had never met. Upon hearing what I do, she immediately asked if I could help a psychic child. I said sure and the connection was made. Peggy called me the very next evening.

"How does this work? Do you want to work with my daughter?" she asked me.

"No, I only work with the parent and teach the parent how to help the child. However, you and I will help the ghostly Annabelle together."

"How can this be? How can I do this? Do you know how many psychics I have asked to help me with this?"

"What matters is that Annabelle needs our help and together we can help her to cross over."

As Peggy and I began to work together, we quickly located Annabelle and for the first time, Peggy could psychically see her as well. That evening, we gave Annabelle a voice: she could finally tell us what happened to her.

"I'm seven, and yes, I am wearing pink pajamas." I explained to Peggy that obviously, these clothes were the clothes she must have died in. This is the story we finally pieced together.

"My family was going home one night, and I guess I was asleep in the back seat of the car when – well - I don't really know what happened. I remember hearing something about a drunk driver who slammed into our car. I don't know how I ended up in this darkness. I was asleep and when I woke up, everything was night, and it never became day. I couldn't find my family and I still can't find them. Why did they leave me? Why don't they come find me? Where's my mommy?"

Annabelle must have died instantly. This poor child never knew what hit her much less if any of her family survived or not. All she knew for sure was that she never 'saw' them again. She looked for them everywhere, but she could never find them, and she missed them terribly. She wanted to join another family, but she couldn't tell us how she happened upon Peggy's family other than she just found Peggy one day and followed her home. She wanted Peggy to be her mom. This was why several times Jocelyn would indicate that Annabelle was hugging Peggy's legs.

Annabelle was angry that Jocelyn was having the life that she was now cheated out of ever having. I think on some level Annabelle realized that she was dead. She eventually came to believe that her family had abandoned her, and it made her dreadfully angry. Annabelle also told us that she used the butcher knife to intimidate Jocelyn into helping her find her family. She somehow realized that Jocelyn could see her, yet the more that Jocelyn tried to ignore her, the more enraged Annabelle became.

As Peggy and I listened to this sad and lonely child our hearts went out to her. Peggy felt her anger toward Annabelle melt away when she realized what this child had been through. What an amazing feeling to be able to offer her the help she had been seeking. Finally, Annabelle herself softened when she realized that we were there to help her. I asked an Angel of Transition to come and assist Annabelle. When this sad and lonely child saw the bright beautiful angel coming for her, she began to cry. She had been so fearful of being alone, abandoned and ignored. She seemed so grateful to have our help and she moved on quite readily when the angel held out her hand to her. Finally, she was no longer angry or afraid and she simply slipped into the light; in an instant, she was gone.

Epilogue

Peggy waited to see if Jocelyn would notice that Annabelle was gone. Jocelyn never saw Annabelle again, and she, Jocelyn seemed much happier and finally at peace.

Peggy realized how difficult it is to protect your child from something you, the parent, cannot see. She also realized how grateful Jocelyn was that her parents believed what she saw. So many children are punished or drugged for telling their parents that they can see a ghost.

We do not know when the accident that took

Annabelle

Annabelle's life occurred or what happened to her mom and her family. It could have happened near this couple's house, which would explain how she found Jocelyn and Peggy. However, we will never really know that answer for sure.

Jocelyn was not necessarily magnetic to ghosts. The challenging reality is that if a child or an adult can see and hear a ghost, the ghost is going to try to get that person to listen. Imagine if you were trying to get someone to help you and no one can hear you or could only hear you in bits and pieces. You would do everything that you could to get that person's attention. This is especially true for children. Children have absolutely no idea what to do at death. Most of them do not understand that they have died. They don't know what 'death' is or what they are supposed to do next. Many adults have the same problem. Any assistance including the simple act of asking an angel to help a child will be deeply appreciated.

At first, I was baffled as to why Annabelle was unable to see her parents if they were alive. However, if Annabelle's parents also died that night, and moved immediately into the light, that would explain why Annabelle could never find them, until she herself crossed over.

With patience, compassion, and a genuine desire for service, this lost and angry ghost child was moved into the Heaven World. The benefit to her was tremendous. However, the unexpected benefit to the living family was that their house no longer felt the oppressive presence of this ghost child. Their own child no longer saw a scary apparition; the rabbit stopped making odd throaty, rumbling sounds, and

Ghost Stories from the Ghosts' Point of View

the cat stopped howling. Finally, this family was able to have a peaceful night's sleep.

Ghost Stories from the Ghosts' Point of View

The Rocket Scientist

Sometimes, karma forces you to step outside of your comfortable paradigm, whether or not you think you want to face it.

Sometimes science cannot provide an answer for a nagging issue that demands your attention.

Sometimes, other people living and dead, shove you into a whole new reality.

And so it was with the NASA rocket scientist who called me to help him with a pesky little problem in his Virginia Beach, Virginia home. When I spoke to him the first time, my conversation went something like this.

"I'm a Rocket Scientist"

"Mrs. Erwin, my name is John Davis, and a friend referred me to you to help me with a . . . well, just a weird problem. Now before we go any farther, I want you to be clear about something: I don't believe in ghosts."

Ghost Stories from the Ghosts' Point of View

"Okay. No problem."

I get it, the guy doesn't believe in ghosts, so why was he calling me? His discomfort was so great I was afraid to say 'boo' to him and yes, pun absolutely intended.

"I'm a rocket scientist. I work for NASA, and I want you to know that I really, really, don't believe in ghosts. All that airy fairy stuff about spirits and haunted houses is just so much New Age garbage in my opinion."

"Sir, truly, I believe you. You don't believe in ghosts. I get it. No problem. However, you called an intuitive, who removes ghosts, so are you sure you have the right number?"

"Of course I have the right number! I'm talking to you about ghosts, aren't I?"

"Okay Mr. Rocket Scientist, I'm listening, so just why did you call me?"

At this point I could readily feel his discomfort. There was definitely a part of him that did not want to have this conversation. However, to his credit, he pushed forward with his 'issue.'

"My friends tell me that my beautiful house at the beach is haunted. I haven't lived there very long but everyone insists it's haunted."

"Well, lots of houses in Norfolk and Virginia Beach are haunted, that's nothing new. All of Virginia is haunted give or take a house here and there. What makes you think your house is haunted? And mind you, I know you don't believe in hauntings, but something has unnerved you or obviously, we wouldn't be having this conversation."

I'm really trying here to help this guy over the

The Rocket Scientist

difficulty he is having even discussing ghosts. Who knew this could be so hard for him?

"I can't seem to start any relationships. Every single time I bring a lady to my house, she gets completely 'weirded out' and races out of my house. Usually none of the women who have come to my home can stand to be here more than a good five minutes."

"Well John, do they tell you why they're leaving so hurriedly? Surely, they give you some explanation."

"One lady said that the house gave her the creeps. Another one said that she felt an angry presence near her. One beautiful woman I really like said that 'someone blew cold air in her face.' She literally ran out of the house. I tried to talk to her, to reason with her, but she slammed the door in my face on her way out."

"Let me guess, you told each of them that there is no such thing as ghosts."

"Of course I did. One woman got so mad at me, that she informed me that she was a high-powered, highly educated executive and that she was not a liar! Then she yelled at me saying that she was not crazy either, and then she stormed out of my house."

"Is that the only sign you have of a ghost; is there any other evidence?"

"Oh, there's more, I think. I can't be sure, but there is this one weird thing that keeps happening. When I leave my house, I make sure that all the lights are off, especially the outside front porch light. Yet, every single night when I return that light is on. I know I didn't turn it on. I even had an electrician look at the switch, and the switch is fine. No one can explain why that light is always on when I return at night. I always turn it off, but the next night, it's on again. Is it possible that I have a ghost? Can you remove the ghost? Do you think I have a ghost? I can't believe I'm even having this conversation!"

I can almost hear him shaking his head at himself.

"I bet this is shaking all of your paradigms about life and death isn't it."

"Shaking's an understatement. Will you help me? I mean can you actually remove them, make them go away?"

"Of course. I'll get back to you."

Those Damn Yankees!

When I 'arrived' at the house to search out the ghost, I met the most amazing soul. What a personality! What a chatterbox! Cora Ann knows she's dead, and she's rather proud of it. She begins chatting with me as if having a psychic visit her is the most natural thing in the world. She informed me that if I thought I was going to get her to leave, I obviously didn't know what a strong woman she is. I was blown away by her brazen approach to life and death. I asked her to tell me why she was still here in this house and did she know she was dead? She was only too willing to talk to me.

"I can see him, he's a'comin' home! I'll put the lamp on for him. I just love him: he's such a right fine man. If I was a bit younger, I just know we'd hit it off. Too bad, though, that I'm dead. Wish I could be in a real body an' be with him. I've watched a lot a people live in this old house, and I really like him best."

"Cora Ann, it's highly unusual for someone to

recognize the fact that they have died. Yet you seem comfortable with being dead, with haunting a living person. Can you tell me when you lived and well, died please?"

"I hated my life! We was so poor and then when the war come, here I be with these five daughters to support and get married off and me with that worthless husband and now there's a war! Those damn Yankees makin' a mess of this countryside. I bet they'd sing a different tune if this war was fought in the North."

"How did you survive once the Civil War started?" I was fascinated with her account of how things were in those critical years from 1860 - 1865.

"When my husband done run off to fight with General Lee, I didn't know how I was gonna' survive but we made it all the way to the end of the war. We never knew when General Lee's boys would come and beg us for food. An iffin' it twern't General Lee beggin' for food, it was them damn Yankees just comin' on in an takin' whatever they wanted.

"Some days I was sure we would starve to death. We had to hide our pigs an' chickens from both armies. They done stole mosta' what we had. By the end, we had no cloth for clothes, nothing to repair our leakin' home and almost no food for the animals.

"We was afraid all the time. Nighttime was the worst, you'all never knows when some renegade soldier would come a callin'. I kept my rifle by my bed and shooed off more than one of them varmints.

"Men and war. Why they gots to be war all the time?

"I even 'member hearin' that that buzzard

Ghost Stories from the Ghosts' Point of View

President Lincoln died. Guess he got what he deserved.

"Guess I didn't. Last thing I remember was goin' out to feed the hogs and collectin' eggs from the one hen we had left in the henhouse when I tripped over a loose board near them hog pens. I remember getting scratched by that ole rusty nail. Put a big ole gash in my leg. But I was so bruised and battered from tryin' to run this tiny farm with just me, and all them girls, that I forgot about it.

"I remember my girls tellin' me I needed to clean up that wound, especially when it started to get all red an angry like. It really hurt. One of my daughters said I was looking pretty yellow around my face and then the next day, I just couldn't speak.

"I guess I went to sleep and then when I woke up, I went out to make breakfast and my girls was cryin'. I told them to hush up, that the war was over, and Daddy'd be back real soon if he hadn't gotten hisself killed. But they just kept on a wailin'. I couldn't figure out why they didn't answer me when I spoke to 'em. Then I watched them go back to my bed and wrap my body in a blanket. The girls took turns diggin'. I reckon it took them a long time to dig my grave. Then they dumped my body in the hole and covered it up with a little lye, so them dogs wouldn't dig me up.

"Now what were my girls gonna do? No momma, no daddy. I surely hope they don't starve to death. . .

"After I died, I kept seeing this beautiful angel comin' for me, but I just told her, that I wanted to have some fun and to leave me alone. I'm stayin' put. It's much more fun to watch the livin' than to have to be livin' in that way, that world.

The Rocket Scientist

"Fact is I don't reckon I really know where I am. What's this place? I don't have to eat or do laundry or worry about those damn Yankees comin' to take food, I can just watch and hang around. This ain't so bad, although it's kinda dark.

"I just hang around this house, but they keep building all kinda buildings 'round here. The house I had got torn down. My daughters got old and one by one, they all died, all made their way toward that pesky light. I watched a couple of them die, but I don't reckon they could see me, they moved on with that bright light pretty quick.

"Not me, I'm stayin' here. This is too much fun. I just love turning on this new-fangled light for this handsome man. Wherever it is he works, it must be nice, 'cause he ain't slopping no hogs in them fancy clothes!

"He keeps trying to bring his lady friends home to do some kissin', but I just keep scarin' um away by touchin' their arm, or appearin' to um, or makin' sure they see me out of the corner of their eye. If they come back, I do more stuff to 'em to make 'em just crazy. I pulled one blonde lady's hair. How do you get hair that color? Shameless hussy! This's my man, and she can't have him! They keep tellin' him that the house is haunted, and he be so prideful, he tells them that he wouldn't live in no haunted house. But he can't explain why I turns on the light for him every night. He knows he turns it off, but I just keeps a turnin' it back on.

"I ain't never leavin' him. He's mine, all mine!"

Opinionated, strong-minded souls in life are opinionated, strong-minded souls in death. This lady had quite an iron will, however, I suspected that there was a part of her that was tired, far more tired than she knew. The fatigue of living through five years of war, of managing to keep five daughters alive must have been exhausting. I felt that with a bit of encouragement, she would readily move into the Heaven World.

"Cora Ann, you do in fact have to move into the light. Your time in this house is over."

"I ain't goin'. I think I love this John Davis and like I done told you it's fun scarin' away his lovlies."

"Do you see this beautiful angel I have brought in for you? He has this wonderful new shawl for your weary shoulders. Can you feel the warmth of the light?"

"I didn't realize I was so cold. And I'm plum tired. I reckon it is time for me to go. I love this angel. Can he help me go all the way into that there light?"

She was willing to make the crossover without difficulty after that. I suspect that on another level, she was lonely. Even though she may have loved a living person, there was only marginal satisfaction in continuing to haunt him. She didn't understand where she was, and she seemed relieved to be moving on to the next point in her soul's existence.

I believe her girls met her as she crossed over. Part of her was relieved to finally be going home and to understand where she was. She smiled as she stepped into the light and slipped away.

Explaining This to the Rocket Scientist

I waited several days, checking on John's house to be sure there was nothing else there. Then I called

The Rocket Scientist

him.

"Ah, Mr. Rocket Scientist, I'm here to report that you did indeed have a very possessive, jealous female ghost. Neither you nor your lady guests are crazy."

"Who is it? How did she get here? Did you order her to leave at once?"

"Well, John, the problem centered around the fact that she was in love with you since the moment you moved into your home. This lady, much like a living person, shall we say, had issues. But the hard part is that her issues went all the way back to the Civil War."

"You mean she's been here since the 1860s?"

"Yes, her name was Cora Ann and she died as a result of a jaundice infection. The irony is that she actually lived through the Civil War supporting five daughters. Lots of women starved to death or were brutalized by marauding, renegade soldiers from both sides. She, however, died in her forties and this property was where her house originally stood when she died in roughly 1865. She has felt possessive of this land. She didn't move into the light, or 'cross-over' because she felt cheated by mortal life and wanted to have more fun experiences. When you moved into the house, she fell in love with you and vowed that you would be hers and no one else's."

"You mean she was trying to possess me?"

"She wasn't trying to possess you in the paranormal sense. She simply wanted a relationship with you . . . as simple as you can call a ghost wanting to have a relationship with you is, in any context. This is why she blew air in the faces of your girlfriends: she wanted to terrify them. She felt this was great 'sport'. She also wanted to see how fast she could get each lady to leave. She told me she turned on the light for you each night so you would somehow know that she was always there for you. Let me assure you, she wasn't any too happy to see me when I came to remove her."

"Did you remove her?"

"Oh yes, she's gone now. I moved her into the correct realm of the Heaven World."

"I guess I realized that the ghost was gone when the light wasn't on for me the last couple of nights when I came home. The house felt oddly empty, like there had been a presence there and now it's gone."

"You may want to invite your girlfriends back and tell them that you did believe them, and you had your ghost spiritually removed. They will appreciate your believing them and taking action. It would be good to invite them back to 'test out the house'."

"Thanks. Maybe I didn't want to believe in ghosts. I'm still not sure how I feel but I am grateful to you for helping me, or her or the situation."

"You're welcome. Always remember that energy is neither created nor destroyed, so the energy of the animation of the human body has to go somewhere at death and that 'somewhere' is into another dimension as a ghost. Even Einstein noted that you cannot 'kill' energy. When your ghost, Cora Ann was assisted in crossing over into the 5th dimension, then she was no longer a ghost in the 4th dimension, and her process of soul evolution and reincarnation, could continue. On a spiritual level, on a cosmic level, you did this lady a wonderful service by enabling her to find God's light."

Epilogue

Whether or not the Rocket Scientist continued to believe in ghosts I will never know. However, he did notice that the front light was no longer on and that he could feel a difference in the energy in his house. Sometimes it is the little things in life that begin to help you to understand how it all works. Maybe he will also open his heart to the plight of a ghost. And just maybe, he will begin to look at Einstein a bit differently.

Ghost Stories from the Ghosts' Point of View

Ghost Stories from the Ghosts' Point of View

The Adorable Red Mazda

Several years ago, I was driving home with my husband when we passed an accident scene. It looked like some poor guy went to the grocery store in his speedy, red, Mazda sports car. On his way home, he apparently accelerated toward the green light, probably wanting to test out his engine. He completely missed that little rise and jog in the road on the other side of the intersection, and slammed, head-on into a power pole.

The police officer stood there looking at this seemingly senseless accident, shaking his head. Had the guy been going a bit slower, he would have had no trouble correcting for the slight shift in the road. He would be on his way home with that now-melting ice cream in the passenger seat of his car.

We have all passed situations where we observe authorities working an accident scene. However, if you are very psychic, you may have a chance to see the accident victim standing there as well, but their perspective will now, unfortunately, be forever changed. And this was the case with this accident scene. The red Mazda was totaled. The ambulance no longer had lights flashing. They were just waiting there until the police could release them and the accident victim's body.

"I'm So Sorry"

What made this scene unique was that I could readily see the deceased driver of the Mazda standing next to his car. I could hear him continually saying how pissed his wife was going to be that he wrecked their new car. He was trying to explain to the police officer that he had either over-corrected or under-corrected for that stupid jog in the road. He went on chatting with the officer about how he was newly married and that he needed to call his wife but for some reason his cell phone didn't work. He kept asking the officer if he could borrow his cell phone, but the officer couldn't hear him. He found himself becoming increasingly irritated. He thought the officer was being rude.

The young man was becoming frantic with the police officer, explaining to him that he had to call his wife. I realized that he thought he was actually talking to the police officer, explaining how this happened. But the poor guy was but a shadow of himself.

"Sir, I have to tell you that unfortunately, you died in this crash. The police officer simply can't hear you." The reality of discovering that you are dead, that the life you thought you were going to live is never going to happen is, emotionally shattering.

"But I can't be dead. I just bumped that phone pole. I have to get home. My wife's waiting for me, for the ice cream. We are going to make sundaes – it's that cool thing that we do on Saturday nights. I look

The Adorable Red Mazda

forward to it all week. You're wrong. The policeman is just being rude. I'm not dead."

It's funny, when you die, you don't think of yourself as becoming a ghost. But that's exactly what happens if you don't move directly into the light when it comes for you. You innocently believe you are still alive. The shock of realizing that you are dead is almost impossible to describe. And so it was with this young man. Shock set in and he just looked at me.

Eventually, the reality of his demise began to sink into his consciousness.

"But you died. Your injuries. . ." He interrupted me with that flash of acceptance.

"I feel terrible that I have disappointed my wife and that I will never get to say good-bye to her. We are going to miss each other so much. She's, my love. I can't bear the thought that some cop is going to knock on my door and tell her. . . . and I'm never going to get to drive my cool car again. I'm not going to get to live a whole life with my brand-new bride. Oh God! I'm so sorry."

He began to grieve for himself, his wife, and his lost life.

"I'm so sorry for this stupid mistake. I can't believe this happened."

Then a new realization struck him.

"Had I just driven a bit slower, done something, anything a bit differently on this trip to the store for ice cream, I would be home now."

Guilt began to set in, and a deep and profound sadness began to envelope him. In one split second, he lost everything that was ever of value to him, his life, his home, his car and most of all, the love of his life. His mortal life was over. In an instant, gone forever because of what he did. This reality created crushing guilt for this poor man.

And it is this agonizing sense of guilt that would have prevented him from crossing over into the light had he not had a little help. Once I requested that Angels of Transition assist him in crossing over, he began to relax. He was beginning the process of accepting his death.

The service of moving him to the Heaven World was truly a most compassionate and important act. Who knows how long he would have continued to stand on that corner lamenting his poor judgment! I also asked the angels to give his body essence assistance. This means that angels apply healing to what would have been his auric field, that etheric template for the physical body. The poor man's chest was crushed. Offering healing to a soul's essence helps their transition because it mitigates some level of soul trauma. It isn't required, but it helps them on the other side. It also seems to mitigate their grief at how they died.

It's ironic that some ghosts cannot see their dead physical structure. It's almost a form of spiritual denial. If you don't see your body, then you believe you must still be in it. Eventually, as the angel guided him home, he did catch a glimpse of his lifeless form and another wave of sadness swept him. And then he was gone.

Epilogue

The critical issue in this story is that the driver of the red Mazda did not stop being who he had been sixty seconds prior to the accident. He was still the same person, the same soul, except that he was no longer attached to his physical body. Anyone can request assistance from the Heaven World for any soul, whether or not you can see him or her. You can also request that his entire essence receive healing no matter the method of death. It's also important to note that guilt can readily cause a soul to indefinitely delay the act of crossing over. Any assistance provided to a ghost is always spiritually beneficial.

Ghost Stories from the Ghosts' Point of View

The Brake Signal

My friend Sandra and I were on a treasure hunt of sorts; we were headed from San Diego to Quartzite, Arizona to scour the crystal vendors there. We were so excited. It's a gorgeous drive over the mountains toward Yuma then up 95 to Quartzite. We had a day or so away from our normal schedule. However, you never know when the dead will need you.

One Angry Man

We had left San Diego on I-8 East and were just past the Sunrise Highway when we joined a long line of stopped traffic. We guessed that there must have been an accident of some sort. As we finally drew closer to the emergency vehicles, we noticed way off in the distance an ambulance leaving, lights flashing.

We were about a mile back, engine off, occasionally coasting down the hill as we inched our way toward the accident. We were chatting, as the jeep ahead of us was able to move several car lengths forward. Sandra released her foot from the brake. As she put her foot back on the break, approaching the rear of the jeep ahead of us, her foot went to the floor. We had no brakes! She threw the car into park and the minivan stopped instantly. We stared at each other. When she took the car out of park, she tried her brakes again, gingerly and they seemed fine. We both knew that we had not imagined the total loss of brakes. We wondered what had happened. Little did we know that the energy of a ghost could affect physical objects, in this case the brakes of Sandra's car.

We were inching closer to the jeep again and then all the traffic was able to merge into one lane and we finally came upon the accident. A little red truck, which had been carrying drywall, somehow skidded and rolled over and over. The entire windshield was smashed in, and the hood of the car was destroyed. There was drywall all over the side of the road. The Border Patrol Agents and police were trying to clean up the road debris. The smashed-up truck was on the flatbed tow truck, about to leave for probably the impound yard.

Sandra asked me if I 'saw' anyone. I looked around and saw the angry truck driver standing there with his hands on his hips looking at his destroyed truck, the drywall all over the road and the giant traffic jam surrounding him. He was livid.

"Damn! I wrecked my truck! Look at the drywall everywhere! I haven't even paid for this! Look, why won't you talk to me! I can't get my cell phone to work, and I need to call my partner. Why won't you talk to me! I've got to figure out how this happened. It

The Brake Signal

happened so fast, all I remember is driving along with my two buddies and the next thing I knew my truck was rolling! I guess I must have swerved to miss something or maybe it was an animal. The best I can guess was that when I swerved, I jerked the wheel too hard to the left and I went up the embankment and the truck just lost it and began to roll."

As I am watching him, I realize that he doesn't understand that when the car rolled, the airbags deployed only one time. With each additional roll, the airbags were useless. Eventually, the steering wheel crushed his chest and one of his rib bones pierced his heart. Death was virtually instantaneous. His passengers were badly battered, but alive.

This poor man was furious. He was outraged, as any mortal person would be facing this situation.

"Officer, I can't believe what a financial catastrophe this is! I lost my truck, the total loss of all of that dry wall that I haven't yet paid for and finally the cost of that tow truck and the injuries I figure my friends have suffered. Where are my friends?"

"Sir, may I help you?" I always ask this gingerly, for the newly dead are in deep shock.

"Who are you? Why don't you look like the others here? Where am I?"

"Sir, when you rolled your truck, you – you didn't make it. Your friends left in the ambulance. I realize that this must be such a shock to you. My job is to help you to cross over."

His own death was not something he had considered. He hadn't come to terms with the accident in the first place, much less the fact that he had died. Once he realized what had really happened, his rage, instead of softening, became even worse.

"I'm not going anywhere! I have things I have to deal with, issues to settle. My life isn't going to be over as long as I have anything to say in this!"

"That's just it, sir, you don't have anything to say about it. Your chest was crushed in the accident and unfortunately your body has already been removed. I wish it could be different, but this is what happened to you."

The hard part is getting him to accept that he will not have a say in anything else regarding this life, ever again. That time is over. Whatever the situations are at a person's death, they are now frozen in time and space and the soul has to accept this. It's done. However, many of them will want to persist in fighting what can never be changed.

The irony of this situation is that souls still have free will in this 4th dimension which is why so many of them choose to hamper the living. However, when there is an opportunity to assist any soul to cross over, this assistance will override that soul's emotional, mortal-based desires.

I brought in an Angel of Transition who offered him assistance. He looked incredulous. He was still in that same state of shock as they simply slipped away with him into the light.

Epilogue

What made this particular case so fascinating was the issue of the brakes in Sandra's car. I realized that when someone is psychically sensitive, they attract some types of energy. In this case I decided that I must have become connected to the rage this ghost

The Brake Signal

was feeling and that this rage went through the brakes, affecting their ability to work properly for a few moments. There was no other explanation. Even though the brake issue immediately corrected itself, it was a tip off to me that there was something spiritually going on at the accident site. This situation also reminded me that we were helping people in the future not to be influenced by the energy of this accident.

When someone dies on a public highway, it is important to help that person to move into the Heaven World. There is poignancy to the situation. When you remove a soul from an accident site, that site then becomes cleared of the energy of a death. If you don't do that, that ghost will still be standing on that spot for years to come, still trying to figure out what happened. For that soul, time and space do not exist. The soul then creates a type of magnetism to that spot. The chilling aspect to this is that you will find that more accidents will take place on that spot. It's the same logic you see when many people commit suicide on a bridge. The souls are still standing there, trying to deal with their sorrow. The energy of that sorrow remains and becomes magnetic to living persons who have that same degree of sorrow.

When you think back to certain intersections that have one accident after the other, you can begin to see why this happens. The same is true for places that have burned. When the energy of fire is never cleared, then when an angry situation comes up, there is always potential for a new fire. This is especially true if someone died in the fire.

The service of helping a ghost to cross over has

the potential of preventing future accidents from happening in that location. Such is the energy of service.

Absolute Control

ust because a challenging personality in your life dies, does not mean you are free from the energetic domination of that person. This person may become a ghost and still influence you. In some situations, this person's death is almost more of an emotional challenge than living with them when they were alive.

Sometimes there is a part of you that knows that you are being haunted by a relative or a friend; but the conscious part of you cannot believe it. So, you deny it.

Eventually the part of you that knows there is 'someone there' simply can't deny it any longer. You bring to consciousness the bizarre, mind-numbing reality that your relative/friend is haunting you.

Now comes the hard part: how do you get your relative to stop haunting you day and night? How do you get someone to believe you and then spiritually help you? Sometimes, the conversation goes something like this.

Finally Taking Action

One evening I received a call from a woman I had

never met. She introduced herself as Helen, and she was the sister of one of my clients. She sheepishly told me that she had had my business card for over a year but had been unable to find the courage to pick up the phone to call and ask for help. She was concerned that this must sound a bit crazy to me.

While I was assuring her that she was not crazy and that I am used to this, I could hear this subtle sense of fear in her voice. It was almost as if I could imagine her wondering if she really was crazy for calling me, for even bringing it up. What if I didn't believe her? Worse yet, what if I didn't believe her and then told her I couldn't help her?

I reassured her that I understood what she was feeling, and I also explained that sometimes there is a reason you can't seem to pick up the phone. I asked her if she felt that every time she went to call me, that something, or someone stopped her. She seemed surprised and excited when I asked her this. My question validated exactly what had been happening. Finally, I could hear some level of relief in her voice. Perhaps she was realizing that this just might work after all.

I asked her how she got my number and she explained that I had helped her brother a year ago when their older brother died. Her living brother in Virginia had continued to urge her to call me, to get help for her debilitating problem. She said her brother felt so much better after their older brother had crossed over into the light after his sudden death.

As we talked, Helen was relaxing bit by bit. She was beginning to explain, without being self-conscious or embarrassed, what was bothering her.

Absolute Control

Sometimes when you are dealing with the supernatural, the living person has to find his or her comfort zone and then begin to tell you what prompted the call. Finally, I asked her what was causing her to be so unnerved. As she hesitated in her answer, I noticed that there was a profound weariness in her voice, as if she had been carrying a terrible burden for a long time and she could bear it no longer.

"It's my mom." Helen said. "She died about ten years ago and - this is difficult to say – but here it is: I believe that she's been haunting me since the day she died." I heard her sigh with relief: she finally got that astonishing statement out.

"Wow, ten years is a long time to feel someone is haunting you. Did you discuss this with any other family members?" I inquired.

"Oh yes, when I finally got the courage to tell my brother, he gave me your card. He told me to 'pick up the phone and call you, DO IT!' he said, but I couldn't until now."

"Out of curiosity Helen, what changed, what made you decide to call me?"

"I finally decided that I can't take it anymore! I haven't had a night's sleep since the woman died. I can't think! I feel like I can't ever escape her. I hear her voice constantly. Oh, and I'm never alone. Who would believe this? It's nuts. I was stressed before she died, but now, it's harder than it has ever been."

I don't think that she had no idea that this flood of emotion, pent up rage, and injustice would come pouring out.

"Why were you stressed before she died? Did you

have to give her constant care? Was it her personality?"

"I wouldn't have minded the constant care, but she never stopped trying to manipulate my every thought, to dictate how my life was supposed to be according to her ideas. I'm almost ashamed to say that I began to imagine what it would be like to not have her in my life. Does that make me a bad person?"

"No, it sounds like you were exhausted from resisting her personality. People like this seem to wear their families out. It sounds like she was/is a pretty controlling personality. I guess that would be an understatement especially if you have a ghost that intimidates this dynamically from the grave."

Helen continued: "You have no idea. My mother was unbelievable. It was always about her. When she was alive, you had to do what she said. I mean, we all knew that she must be obeyed! No matter what! If I didn't do exactly what she said, she made my life hell and now for me, even in death she's making my life hell."

"Time to get to work. I need your permission to see what I can find."

"You have my permission to look and see if you can find her. Thank you. You, ---- you have no idea what this means to me."

"Then I'll get to work and get back to you as soon as I can."

Malevolent, Mischievous Millie

I quickly made contact with her ghostly mother, Millie. Sometimes it's amazing how surprised some ghosts are that I can see them and converse with

Absolute Control

them. Some apparitions absolutely relish operating invisibly with total power over their intended targets. This woman obviously enjoyed her ghostly reality.

"Hello Millie."

"Oh my, can you see me?"

"Yes, I can see you quite clearly. I've been sent here to help you cross over into that beautiful light that I bet you've seen many times."

Millie, ever confident, feeling powerful in this situation calmly responded.

"I have no intention of leaving my daughter. I told her not to call you. I was able to get her to put that phone down every time but, obviously, not this last time. I'm going to be with her until she dies. She needs me and she can't manage without me. Because you know, she doesn't fully have the intelligence or the judgment to live her life without me."

Millie's arrogance was just as her daughter had described.

"Do you talk to Helen when she's sleeping?"

Millie was quite proud of this part. "Yes, that's when I do my best work. I can prepare her for the next day. She thought that when I passed on that I would leave her, but I didn't. I also discovered that it's wonderful being out of that old decrepit body and never having to sleep. I can travel all over the place so quickly!"

"Millie, have you ever considered that your daughter is 55 years old? When does she get to grow up?"

Millie was smugly proud of her ability to haunt her daughter.

"She grew up into a person who needs to be controlled. That's my job as her mother."

I decided to offer her another view of her actions.

"You do realize that in this state, you're incurring karma for influencing your daughter's free will?"

"Who cares about that? She's my daughter and she will obey me!"

"Well, this is probably going to come as a bit of a shock to you, but once you're dead, you don't get to control her anymore. She gets to live her life without you. That's one of the reasons for your death: your daughter can now approach life in her own way. She's entitled to be free to choose how she wants to live her life. That's how it works."

"Well, I don't like it. Besides, you can't tell me what to do. Remember I have free will too!"

"Well, Millie, you do, and you don't. When you get to the point where you are harming another person and the living person decides to stop you, then that person's rights trump yours. My job is to ensure that you cross over and allow the Divine Beings on the other side to guide you in this next segment of your non-mortal existence."

"Oh really? Hah! What makes you think you can force me to cross anywhere? I won't go. That's all there is to it. I simply won't go, and you can't make me! So there."

I shook my head. Was I talking to a woman who died at age 87 or a spoiled rotten five-year old?

"Pretty much, you no longer have a choice. See that big angel over there? Well, I've called him to assist us, and it's my job to direct him to escort you to the Heaven World, which is exactly what I'm doing

Absolute Control

right now."

I nod to the angel patiently standing by.

"It's time to go Millie. Say good-bye to your daughter. Your days of controlling her are over."

"But I don't want to go! I WON'T GO!!!"

Millie is facing having her will thwarted for the first time in either dimension, and she seems stunned by this turn of events. But the light is divine and the energy of the divine melts even the most stubborn soul.

"Look over there. Do you see that light? Do you recognize anyone?"

"Oh my, is that my grandmother? She's calling for me! Oh, I've missed her so much, and my dad's over there waiting for me, too. I had no idea."

"It's time. Go with the angels now Millie."

She crosses over with delight, and never looks back. The angel smiles at me, and then he transitions with her into the Heaven World, and the scene fades.

Epilogue

The next evening, I called Helen and shared with her how things went with her mom. Helen was so excited to hear all of the details. I was curious how she was feeling with her mother no longer haunting her day and night.

"Hi Helen! How are you feeling?"

"Oh my God, I can't believe how much better I feel! Last night I had my first peaceful night's sleep in a long, long time. Do you know what it means to me to have a whole night's sleep?"

"Believe me, I do. What else have you noticed?" I was most curious to know what she had experienced or was no longer experiencing with the departure of her mother. For some people the action of moving on a haunting spirit is life changing.

"I felt like my whole body was suffering from aches and pains. I believed I was aging overnight. It was horrible. The pains in my knees and hips are now completely gone. Was that my mother's doing?"

"I believe it was. Did she have arthritis?"

"Yes, she had terrible arthritis in her knees and her hips bothered her constantly. Did you really move her on? Was it difficult? Did she give you a hard time?"

"Difficult, no, did she give me a hard time? I pretty much knew that anyone that controlling would be resistant to changing how she had been doing business in life and in death. Yes, she refused, believing that you couldn't possibly function without her. She also admitted that she directly influenced you not to call me those previous times. It must have taken a lot for you to eventually pick up that phone."

"Oh, that was so my mother. She was impossible! Is it wrong of me to be glad that my mother's dead and now finally gone?"

I found myself smiling at this comment. We grieve those we have adored differently than those souls who have challenged us in life. It is not unusual to find relief in the passing of a person who has been incredibly difficult.

"I had her escorted to the Heaven World so she will not be back to bother you. Crossing over is a one-way door. The only way for her to return is to reincarnate as a baby. She probably won't be doing that for a while."

"Is it wrong to be so happy about this? Sometimes

Absolute Control

I have such conflicting emotions."

"Absolutely not! And I do have some idea what you have been through. My controlling mother-in-law threatened to haunt my husband and me before she died. When she died, I absolutely ensured that she was moved on. It was my last compassionate act for her. Believe me, I understand."

Helen was indeed a powerful bundle of conflicting emotions. We all believe that we have to love our parents, but what do we do when we have a domineering, controlling and abusive parent? How do you love such a toxic personality? I've been asked repeatedly if it's wrong to be happy when that person finally dies. I refuse to believe it is wrong to be relieved when you are no longer being tortured.

"Your mom was controlling and abusive. Probably, in her mind, she felt that love meant control, not independence. When you truly love someone, you love that person enough to let him or her go. Your mother's entire identity was tied up in controlling you. Without that, she had no other identity, no other sense of purpose. In reality she was quite insecure. Now you can live a whole life and enjoy it."

"Thank you so much for helping me. Was this any help to her? What happened when she crossed?"

"Her grandmother and her dad met her, and she was thrilled to see them. This is a situation where everyone benefits from your courageous action of requesting help. In a way, you also set her free. She can make far more spiritual progress in the Heaven World than she could ever make haunting you day and night."

"Thank you, perhaps someday you will know what

this has meant to me. I cannot begin to describe the profound sense of freedom I'm feeling. I'm finally alone in my body! I couldn't explain this to anyone. I just know that now I can be my own person. Thank you so much."

"You're welcome, Helen."

Their Accusing Eyes

When you study healing, when you study the humanity, and the emotion of the human spirit, there is a tragic truth that is eternally operative: guilt will always seek punishment.

The punishment that a soul seeks is in direct proportion to the volume of guilt that lives within a person, living or dead. The following story is a classic case of this universal truth. I sincerely hope that your heart goes out to this woman.

"Quick! Wake up!"

The demanding phone insists that I answer it. It's six in the morning as I glance at the clock. Who can possibly be calling me at this hour? I take a deep breath and pick up the phone. In the strange world in which I live, I never have any idea what insistent issue will claim my attention. I never know what the next phone call will bring.

The frantic, adamant voice on the other end of the line was one of my closest friends, Anita.

"Tina, wake up quickly! You have to help me, my divorce lawyer has been haunting me all night long and I need you to do something to her, for her, or with her immediately. I'm not sure what you need to do, but you have to get her to stop right now!"

Anita is one my dearest friends; I have known her for at least twenty years. She has been divorced for at least five years, so I was surprised to hear her tell me about her divorce attorney. I knew that for her to call me this early, something serious was happening to her.

"Anita, did you tell me your divorce lawyer was even ill? Did I already know that?"

"No, not sure I mentioned it to you, but yes, she's been quite ill. She had breast cancer. One day she was fine and the next she had this aggressive breast cancer. I visited her in the hospital. It was so sad. I didn't know what to say to her. I couldn't believe it. I remember sitting with her and telling her how much good work she had done for me, and how much I appreciated her dedication to her profession. I remember her simply turning her head and crying.

Her husband and two daughters were there. I tried to get her to accept healing, but she refused. She said she didn't want that. I got the impression that she had accepted her fate."

"I do remember your mentioning this. I just didn't realize that she had passed away. I'm so sorry to hear that. But how do you know she's haunting you?"

"I don't know how to explain it exactly, but I can feel her presence. It's as if she's trying to tell me something I can't hear. Tina, she kept me up all night! I don't even understand how this works, but I can tell you that she's here. I feel a sense of her, like she's standing beside me trying desperately to get my attention. Will you please talk to her? Her name's Lydia."

"Yes, I'll check into it and make a connection with her. I'll get back to you."

"Don't You Get It? I'm Angry!"

I was able to connect to Anita's ghost pretty quickly by remote viewing her bedroom. Lydia wasn't hard to find. I could see her standing by Anita's bed. I realized right away that she could see me as I spoke to her.

"Hello Lydia. Anita asked me to come and talk to you. She seems to think you are in some level of distress. Can you tell me why you're with her?"

"I love Anita not just as my client, but as my friend, and I was trying to tell her why I died. She couldn't seem to understand why I was so ill. She just didn't get it."

"Did your family get it? Did your family understand why you left? Did they have any understanding why you had breast cancer?"

"There's no way I could hope to explain to my husband, to my daughters why I was leaving. I knew I was dying. I deliberately refused healing. How do you tell your family that you are ready to die, that you are glad to be leaving? It was horrible. I love them so much, but I couldn't bear life anymore."

"Have you visited your daughters? Can you see their grief at your passing?"

"Yes, I can feel it. This whole thing is my fault. It's such a nightmare. I can't believe I'm having this conversation with you. And no, I never tried to explain this to my girls or my husband. I don't want to dump my stuff on them. Now, I guess as a ghost, I don't even want them to feel my despicable presence."

Perhaps the truth was I was still having a hard time understanding why she was with Anita in the first place. I would have thought that she would have been with her children or her husband trying to explain to them why she died. It was obvious to me that she knew exactly why she was in this position. This was not a woman who did not know her mind. There wasn't much she didn't do without a focused reason. Something was really bothering her. I wanted to offer her some solace so I discretely brought in an angel who would be standing by to help her eventually transition into the Heaven World. I knew she would be able to see that angel. Her reaction to the angel would tell me a great deal about her state of mind.

"Lydia, your girls are grieving their mother and that is a great deal of 'stuff' on them, especially in high school. Not to mention how much your husband must miss you. I get the impression that you're not visiting him either. You seem cut off from the love of your family and friends, as if you have completely cut yourself off from love.

"I want you to understand that you are never separated from God, from the love inherent in the divine. The angel beside you is offering you comfort so that you can begin to have that feeling that you are loved before you begin your transition into the Heaven World."

"Oh no. No way! I'm not going anywhere with that angel. Yes, I can see him, but you, you send him back

Absolute Control

where he came from. Don't you get it? I'm . . . I'm angry and no angel's going to help me get over it. So just send him away!"

It isn't unusual for a soul to refuse an angel. However, the reason for refusal is always significant. In her case I knew she would eventually tell me if I could get her to soften her anger at herself.

"Alright, I'll ask the angel to stand by, but he's not leaving. Tell me, Lydia, what were you trying to tell Anita?"

"I was trying to tell her how sorry I am that I successfully engineered her divorce. Her divorce was the hardest for me of all the ones I did. I can't explain it. It just tore me up inside."

Lydia looked down at where her feet would have been, and I could see her shoulders hunched over, as if she had the weight of a thousand 'sadnesses' upon her.

I decided that she needed a different kind of care, a unique kind of spiritual assistance, so I requested a child angel to come in and stand by her.

"Why was Anita's divorce the hardest? You did a great job with that divorce. You helped her so much. Because of you, she has a reliable income, and her child is cared for as well. She depends on that every month and thanks to you she has it. She always spoke so highly of you. She noted how fair, how balanced you were when you approached each dicey bump on the road to her divorce. Obviously, you were quite a successful attorney. My understanding is that you were one of the most successful divorce attorneys in San Diego."

"DON'T YOU GET IT? DON'T YOU SEE? I'm a

terrible person!"

"No, I don't get it. I don't see. Tell me. Tell me what has made you so angry and why in the world you would consider yourself a terrible person?"

I quietly had the child angel come up and slip her hand in Lydia's hand and then look up at her with love and compassion. A child angel is not as visually intimidating as a full-sized angel, and I felt that this woman needed a different kind of spiritual assistance.

"Yes, I was a good attorney. I was a damn good attorney! Yes, I was successful. I was so hugely successful that I managed to engineer literally hundreds of divorces. HUNDREDS of DIVORCES! In most of those divorces where there were children, I watched as all of those children saw the love they had for one parent or another utterly betrayed! BETRAYED! Those kids believed that their parents would love one another, and I 'successfully' participated in making sure that they would be divorced, separated, living apart. I saw hundreds of kids look up at me when the divorce was final as if I was somehow at fault. Ultimately, I know they believed it was my fault that their parents would never get back together!"

"But you did what you were asked to do, what needed to be done to end what could be a variety of situations from all kinds of abuse to abandonment or mental cruelty."

Lydia has now looked down at the child angel and taken her tiny glowing hand. The innocence and kindness from this child are so powerful, it reduces Lydia to tears. Finally, the emotional release I was looking for begins, as she starts sobbing. She accepts

Absolute Control

the child's comforting presence and seems to be releasing her pent-up anger, rage and what I believe is the ironic cause of her death: her guilt at doing an exceptionally good job for all of her clients.

"I was the best! And the best was a dream destroyer! I shattered the dreams all those kids had that they would ever have a happy home, that their parents would ever get back together. Do you know how many kids looked at me with such sad eyes in my office? There was nothing I could do to comfort them. I let parents say some of the cruelest things one parent can say about another in front of these kids.

If the walls of my office could talk, well the walls wouldn't talk, they would cry, but I never cried. I just began to feel more and more guilt, guilt for destroying the belief those kids had in their mom and dad, in marriage, in living and loving. I'm a terrible person!" Her outpouring of grief and regret continued.

"Lydia, you are not a terrible person. You were a good lawyer. You did your job. The hard truth is that some people need to be divorced. Sometimes the karma between two people is over and they have to separate from each other. This isn't right or wrong or good or bad: it's simply a fact of mortal life. Your ability to help two people successfully divorce may have saved the life of many an abused woman and her children. Perhaps some of the sadness you saw was the tremendous disappointment these children had in the behavior of their parents. You felt their sadness because you are a sensitive person, but you were not responsible for the behavior of their parents. Doing a good job, can mean that you have to walk through a great deal of darkness when you deal with people's volatile emotions during a divorce. The tragedy in your case is that you couldn't shed the intensity of darkness that infected people divorcing. Perhaps it was that darkness that caused your breast cancer. You took to heart the grief those families felt when the love between two people is betrayed. You may be a lawyer, but you were a far more sensitive lawyer than you may have given yourself credit for being.

"If you were so disturbed by your job, why didn't you change jobs? You could have left the profession."

"I thought about it. I tossed it around but by then, I had already found a pretty large lump in my breast. Leaving my profession wasn't going to make my guilt any less at this point. The damage I rightly or wrongly believed I had done to all those kids was already a reality. I guess you could say I gave up. What was the point of living after that?"

I realized that reminding her of her duty to her own children and husband would not bring her any solace. Her blame over doing an unfortunately good job at her job would not be any less when she considered that her guilt also took her away from her loving family. I realized that she never shared her guilty beliefs about herself with any of her family members. She was powerfully alone with her guiltiness, and it broke her heart. Many times, breast cancer is the symptom of an exceptionally sad heart and that sadness, can readily be caused by some type of guilt.

"I think I understand that you were trying to tell Anita you were sorry. I'll let her know if you like. I do know that she never blamed you. She was grateful that you handled her case so professionally. Perhaps that is small comfort. Ultimately, you blamed yourself and it became so toxic inside of you that it created a way for you to leave."

"Yes, please, let her know. So, do you see why I'm not worthy of God loving me? Despite what you have said, I still feel that I am a love destroyer! I can't ever go into that light, I'm so guilty, and there's no way God can forgive me."

And with this statement, her gut-wrenching sobs would have broken anyone's heart had they heard them. Now, several angels joined the child angel in offering her their gentle compassion. They nodded to me that they were ready to take her to the Heaven World for healing.

"Lydia, God has already forgiven you. Perhaps you cannot see your own goodness, but let me assure you, God can see it. God has always seen it. Your transition will enable you to receive not just the love that will heal your heart, but also the wisdom and guidance to understand the life more fully you have just lived. I have brought these angels here to guide you home into that warm, welcoming, loving light. There you will get to heal your broken heart."

"Why would you do this for me? I'm not worthy."

"God's love isn't conditional. God's love is absolute. It's there for all of us whether or not we ever think we are worthy of it. The Light of God's love is the hope of redemption, of healing, of learning. Please allow this wonderful divine love to come to you. As for me, it's not up to me to judge you or anyone else. My job, and my pleasure, is to assist you in finding your way home. It's time. These beautiful angels will guide you."

Finally, she gave me a brave smile and turned with her escorts into the light and then, she was gone.

Epilogue

Lydia's guilt was so profound, so toxic that it literally created a cancer inside of her. She was a good person in a heartbreaking field. Someone has to do that job and that job can be a profound service to those in a difficult situation. However, few if any, of us ever give a thought to the emotional toll that is taken on a divorce lawyer. Most people are so focused on their own particular drama that he or she would never even think of what their lawyer might be going through. Nor would they think that an attorney would have an emotional reaction to any family's divorce drama.

I called Anita to let her know that her friend had transitioned into the Heaven World and that she finally seemed to find some level of peace. Anita seemed greatly relieved and noted that she could feel almost instantly when Lydia had crossed over. Anita noted that her house felt peaceful again. She told me that it never occurred to her that Lydia was distressed by her job. However, she was glad to know that her friend was finally at peace.

Perhaps it was Lydia who experienced the most severe haunting. Imagine seeing hundreds of children with tear-stained faces leaving her office, day after day, week after week. The emotional toll on Lydia was simply overwhelming. In the end, it was those children who emotionally haunted her, literally, to death.

We would each be wise to remember that no

Absolute Control

matter how difficult a situation, we can each reach out and receive the love of the Father in Heaven. At the end of our lives, we may wonder how well we embraced each situation that confronted us, how much we loved one another and how much we grew inside as a person.

However, how much we loved and how much we were loved by others, at the end of the day, at the end of a lifetime are the most important elements of anyone's life.

Their Accusing Eyes

The Intruder

John Hollister and his wife Katy bought a big 4,000 square foot house in a gorgeous gated community in San Diego, California.

They thought they knew all the facets of purchasing what the neighborhood called 'the house from hell.' It wasn't like they had no idea how bad it was.

They did realize that something horrendous must have happened there.

They knew that the previous owner left his wife alone in that house for days on end and she went utterly mad, but no one knew why. She became so insane, that she had to be committed.

When John and Katy bought the house, they knew that the walls and floors were covered with blood, urine, and feces. They found terrible scratches in the walls on the ground floor.

When the couple looked at buying the house, it had already been for sale for five years. No one wanted that house or would take it on: it had a horrible reputation. However, this couple was sure that with a little work, they could simply clean it up.

They spent at least $100,000 and gutted the entire house down to the studs. He was a builder, and she was a decorator. They poured their time, energy, money, and love into what they hoped would be their dream home.

Tragically, however, they had no idea that no amount of soap and water, paint and fabric would change the energy enough to remove the terrifying things that existed there psychically.

What started out to be their dream home became their own little house of horrors.

The following story shows that often, profound, and toxic predecessor energy can overwhelm a family, as this unusual encounter so tragically illustrates.

John Comes to Call

One evening I turned around to see a man standing in my bedroom! You can well imagine my shock at seeing my neighbor standing there in his heavily soiled shirt and shorts looking like he had just lost his best friend.

"Can you help me?" He seemed desperate and at the same time apologetic.

"What are you doing here John? You scared me half to death! How'd you get into my house?" I was trying to get my heart to calm down so that I could coherently speak to him. It was immediately obvious to me that he did not mean me any harm but what a surprise! John tried to explain.

"Well, I watched you from the street. Actually, I've been watching your house for several days. I had no idea you were, well 'bright'."

The Intruder

"Bright?" I had no idea what he meant by this.

John continued. "You know, well, 'bright', like all 'glowy'."

"What do you mean - me or my house?"

"Well, sort of both. What I mean is that you seem so bright to me that I felt that if I explained my situation to you that maybe, you would help me. I really need you to help me."

"You realize John, you can't be here. You don't just enter someone's house without knocking or asking. This goes beyond creepy!"

"Yes, I know this must seem unusual to you, but you know I need your help, and I'm sorry if I upset you but I need help with my wife."

"What's wrong with your wife and have you visited her since the accident?"

"Well, I have visited my wife, but she ignores me. It's so frustrating. No matter how much I plead with her she refuses to listen to me. I need her to leave that house and you know how awful that house is, don't you?"

"I know what the gossip is about the house: that it has a chilling feeling inside it, that the first woman who owned it went utterly insane and that no one would purchase it for at least five years. I also understand that there is something basically evil about that house and that it was the house that drove that woman crazy. She did have to be committed. But honestly, what do you want me to do about it?"

"I want you to go to my house and talk to Katy, tell her that she has to leave that dangerous place. Tell her that you spoke to me and that I told you that the house is evil, and that she just has to get out. Tell her

I sent you. I just know she'll listen to you."

John's frantic attitude made my initial startled reaction begin to thaw, so to speak. I began to appreciate the desperation he must have felt and how concerned he was about his wife in what, for her is a terrible situation.

"Ok, perhaps I think I know why it's dangerous, but why do you think it's dangerous?" I needed him to tell me what he was seeing, feeling, and sensing, from his perspective.

"There are, you know, 'things' in the house. They live there."

"You mean vermin? Rats? I need you to be specific. I want to know exactly what you've seen."

The poor man looked towards his feet in an embarrassed way.

"There are these little dark guys. Do you know what I mean? God, I hope you know, 'cause if you don't know, who else can I turn to? Who else can I explain this to? I'm desperate! You have to know!"

"You mean, the little three-foot tall devil-like beings?"

He was greatly relieved that I had some idea what he was talking about.

"Little torturers would be more like it. I refused to believe it at first. I'm a rational kind of a guy. I didn't believe in ghosts or anything paranormal. But no matter what we did to that house, they were still there. We redecorated, repainted, and we repaired everything, but the problems started the first week we moved in. We had night after night of no sleep. I felt like I was going crazy. I didn't want to tell my wife because I didn't want her to think I was going nuts. I

The Intruder

guess I did begin to go a little batty. What I didn't realize was that she was seeing them too. Funny, we never saw ghosts, only these terrifying black creatures that would come at us and once the lights were out, we could --- we could actually feel them. They touched us."

John shivers at the thought of this. I felt my skin crawl. Imagine being touched be these little devils. I shuddered remembering their red beady eyes and their sooty, filthy three-foot bodies.

"Then the fights started: we couldn't agree on anything. Finally, the arguments turned vicious. I had to leave the house more and more frequently so that our fights wouldn't turn physically violent. I couldn't stand it anymore and I turned to drugs. I guess Katy turned to alcohol to escape them. It got worse from there. Our finances went into the toilet. Finally, we both began to be able to see those little dark guys out of the corner of our eye. Eventually we could see them all the time. I had trouble determining what was real anymore. I guess I thought that death would be my only escape..."

"But death is no better than life, is it?"

"No, it isn't. If I had only known that I might not have shot myself last week. Now, now it's worse. They physically pull on me all the time! They torture me constantly. The only relief I could find was standing in front of your house and feeling the light. That's the only time they leave me alone. I felt that you'd be the one mortal person I could talk to who might understand, provided that you could see me and then actually hear me. Did you know that when you're dead no one hears you?"

Ghost Stories from the Ghosts' Point of View

"John, I'm so sorry about this situation. I do know that few people hear those who have died. I can feel how upset you are. I can also both see and hear you, and my heart goes out to you. I do appreciate what a horrific situation you're in, but you have to understand, I can't just go down and talk to your wife."

"Well, they do it on TV. The psychic goes down, knocks on the door, and talks to some family member and everyone's okay after that. Why can't you do that?" John demanded.

"Because it isn't that simple. People can become unnerved by such a conversation and at this point, I'm not sure what kind of an emotional state your wife is in since your suicide. Does your wife have any idea that there is something negative there?"

"Yes, actually she does. She brought in a Catholic priest to do an exorcism, but he was ineffectual. Then she hired some Mormon minister to do the same thing and he was worthless. I was standing there watching these guys. None of them could see me. They had no idea what they were doing. They burned a little incense and some sage. I guess one guy said he used special prayers. Nothing any of them did made any difference to these little devil things. I could feel her panic. I think she knew that these little devils drove me to suicide."

"So, when each of these clergymen were unsuccessful, what did she do next?"

"I couldn't believe it. She actually called the priest back in and insisted that he do a better job, but he also failed. She's so depressed and I don't know how to help her. That's why I thought if you could just talk to her, she might believe you. Why can't you try?"

The Intruder

"I can't do that because frankly, she is in a very, very fragile state right now. Her husband committed suicide barely ten days ago. She's broke, she feels powerless and then she has a friend knock on her door and tell her that her house is overrun by these little dark guys and oh, your dead husband sent me to warn you. No, it really works much better on TV. In real life, you can only do that on very rare occasions."

"What am I going to do?"

"You're going to cross over into the Heaven World, and I can help you with that."

"I don't think so. How can God forgive me? I feel so guilty that I killed myself. I caused her so much more pain and I can't imagine that God would welcome me after all of this. I can't abandon my wife in such a terrible situation. I have to do something to help her."

"And you will. I'll help you to cross over. Then once you're there, angels will guide you in how to approach your wife in the dream/sleep state. Then you'll be able to help her to realize that she has to leave that house."

"If it doesn't work, can I come back and talk to you?"

I found myself deeply touched by John's overwhelming concern for his wife.

"Yes, of course you can, but honestly, I've never had anyone come back. This works whether you believe it or not."

I didn't tell him that crossing over is a one-way door. Besides, no one ever wants to return to the previous hell of the 4th dimension.

"I guess I do want to go, it's so lonely on this side.

I've been cold all the time. This light you talk about, this crossing over, does it hurt when it happens?"

"No, John, it doesn't hurt at all. It's simply the most wonderful welcome home. There is love and light and hope where you're going."

As the conversation continues, the Light of Transition begins to appear for him.

"Is that light I see coming for me? Oh my God, is that my mom? I can see my mom! I didn't think I would ever get to see her again. I'm so sorry I killed myself. I wish I had understood what was happening in our house, but I was so tired, so gray feeling all the time."

John vacillated between being remorseful for his actions toward himself, concern for his wife and yet hopeful that he could be forgiven and be with his loved ones again. Hope is a powerful opportunity.

"Once I committed suicide, I didn't think anyone would ever forgive me. But there's my mom. That light is growing brighter, and it feels like I'm being pulled toward it. I'm finally feeling warmer as I get closer to this warm welcoming light."

John's shoulders began to sag as he relaxed into the reality that he could finally return home.

"I think I'm ready to go, but I'm still worried about my wife. You have to assure me that this'll work."

"Yes, John, I'm absolutely positive."

"Then, thank you, I - I just wish I had known before I died that you were here."

"I understand what you're saying. It works the way it works, John. Once you cross over, I'll ask that angels and other Light Beings help you to assist your wife. You have my word."

The Intruder

I watched, as John seemed to merge with the light. Ironically, as he entered the realm of light that is the Heaven World, his self-inflected wounds vanished, his bloody clothes were no longer soiled with the evidence of his despair and his entire soul body seemed to glow with love.

And with that he was gone.

I had found it so sad seeing him floating there wearing the bloody clothes he wore in death. I felt so much better knowing that he was with those who can love and heal him of his sadness.

I was also glad that he was so dedicated in finding help for his wife despite how much he had startled me by appearing in my bedroom. One of the spiritual laws that seemed to operate here is that as you seek to help someone else to heal, so are you also healed. The interesting irony here was that as he was seeking to help his wife, he in turn received the divine assistance he desperately needed.

Epilogue

This encounter took place in the mid 1990s. During that time, I was learning how to help both the dead and the living in difficult situations. However, this one encounter gave me a real understanding for the frustration a dead person can feel when the soul desperately wants to help their living relatives. It was the first time I ever had a ghost go to this length to seek me out to help a family member.

John did cross over into the Heaven World and seemed to find great peace after that. However, you may wonder if he was ever able to speak to his wife in the dream/sleep state. Well, all I know for sure is that the very next morning, his wife left the house and vowed never to return. To this day she has never set foot on that property. She sent someone else in to pack her things. She put the house on the market and had someone else supervise her move. Emotionally, she had a hard time recovering from the many layers and dimensions of her ordeal after the suicide of her husband and the torture she felt living in that house.

So, what happened to the house over the last ten years? After several years of it being for sale, another couple bought it and they had two family members die of illnesses. They also sold the house to another family and the young wife almost died of problems with a valve in her heart. They sold the house to the current owners.

It was those current owners who finally allowed me to clear it. I remember asking them how their house felt, considering all that had happened there. Surprisingly, no one else had mentioned the home's history to them. I was unfortunately, or fortunately the one to share the home's tragic tale with them and it was at that time that they gave me permission to clear it.

What I discovered was that this particular property had once been a swamp with a tremendous amount of stagnant energy. That stagnant energy became increasingly evil feeling as time progressed. This negative stagnant energy has a tendency to attract people with the same negative feeling within them. Compounding the problem, somewhere in the recent past, someone had performed a dark ritualistic action on that property, be it with Ouija, Tarot, or the deliberate practice of black magic. When I cleared it, I

The Intruder

removed all of those little devils and gave healing to the entire property. After that, the house and property finally felt peaceful.

So far, the house has not changed hands, no further terrible things have taken place there and no family members of the current owners have died tragically. The land is finally at peace . . . and, I like to believe that John is finally at peace as well.

The Intruder

The House of the Underground Railroad

This tragic story takes place in Suffolk, Virginia. The request came from a pair of homeowners who kept hearing various sounds in their house. The sounds weren't specific, not sounds that could be accounted for in the mortal world we call present time. The wife feared that their home was haunted. This couple had a new baby, and the wife was afraid that perhaps the ghosts, if they were in fact ghosts, could harm their new child.

The husband was not totally convinced of this ghost concept, but he didn't want to take any chances, so he seemed to go along with his wife's request for a clearing.

The couple also described a series of nasty encounters with all of their neighbors. They felt that perhaps the sounds indicated that something had happened on the property that would make things in the neighborhood feel negative. I have seen this in other situations. Sometimes where something terrible has taken place in the past on a large section of property, say many dozens of acres, that toxic energy can definitely affect the current land area. Often times, the energy of positive or negative events does not know a specific boundary.

I agreed to take a look.

Three Very Long Nights of Anguish

Sometimes when you remote view a location, it takes time to sift through the stacks of time to find that precise stack which is having the greatest influence on a particular piece of property. This is not a quick process. In this case, it took three very long, stressful nights of work.

When I finally located the specific stack of time having the greatest influence on this property, I immediately found myself observing a bloody ambush during the Civil War. At least several dozen acres of property were involved in this skirmish, which seemed to be endlessly raging on and on in a place of no time and space. What this means is that the energy is so powerful that it keeps replaying over and over. This was a classic case of toxic and active predecessor energy.

The location of this couple's property also showed another house that had existed on this property at the time of this battle. This house was a two-story burned-out shell of an 1840s vintage home that was used by the Underground Railroad during the Civil War to smuggle run-away slaves to the Northern and Western United States. It would be hard to imagine the sheer volume of fear alone that would have inhabited that house over the months and years of the Civil War. Slave after slave would have huddled in the dark places in that house, hoping to avoid detection

The House of the Underground Railroad

by the Confederate Army. Probably thousands of slaves hoped and prayed they could be rescued and smuggled to safety. Perhaps some of them made it.

As this particular scene opened up, I found a desperate slave family huddled in a corner of the house. The head of the family, an enormous black man, stepped up to address me. He seemed to be covered in sweat, his filthy clothes were a visual testimony to his dire situation. His manner was most respectful, humble, and fearful. At the same time, he seemed oddly relieved to see someone who had the promise of helping him. I could see a black woman and a boy about seven years old huddled behind him. Near them I could see other men, their gaunt faces mute testimony to the destruction of the Civil War. I asked the man how they got there.

"We had heard of this here house, that you could escape to and then get hep. One day, we was out in the fields when we decided we was gonna' make a break for it. Then we all went into the woods by the field. My woman and boy jus' slipped away into the woods with me. Other folks in our slave house told us about this here house that we could stay in 'til other white folk could come find us an hep us escape to the North."

"You must have been so afraid as you left that field!"

"Oh ma'am, you gots no idea! We was scared that iffin' the South done lost the war, then our lives was gonna be worse. We was hopin' for a better life someplace North. Our boy was wide-eyed an too scared to speak to us. We made it by runnin' all night to this here house. We kept waitin' for the folks who was supposed to help us escape. I 'member lookin' and awatchin' out for them."

"What happened? Did they ever come?"

"Naw, what happen to us was not somethin' we coulda' thought. Whilst we was huddled in the house near mostly dark, we heard riders 'acomin' toward us. We was terrified that it was General Lee's boys 'cause that woulda' been real bad. But it weren't no Rebs, it was Yankees. A whole bunch a Yankee soldiers surrounded the house. Then it began to rain somthin' terrible and they come into the house to be a little drier and they done found us. They wasn't too big a group. I reckon nary more than 50 soldiers. We all shared the space and we hoped that havin' them there would be better protection for us, but it sure didn't turn out that way."

"What happened?"

"What happened was that we was all trying to stay dry in part of this here house with a roof left and I guess we kinda fell asleep. I gots no idea how long we was asleep. Alls I remember was the sound. I ain't never gonna' forget that scream that made my blood run cold.

The sound was a whole bunch a Reb soldiers attackin' us. They'd been tracking those Yankees for I don't rightly know how long. Once they found them, they waited in that pouring rain in the night for them to settle down. Me, my woman an boy had tried to settle down to sleep too, when dem Rebs came out of the night screamin' an hollerin' like some devils from hell. My woman starts 'ascreamin' 'Aw Lordy, they's comin! They's comin!' They come a hootin' and shootin' like crazy. Afore we knowed it, all dem Yankees was

The House of the Underground Railroad

dead. I couldn't believe it. How'd they kill 'em all so fast?

"Lady, dem Rebs killed every one of dem Yankees! They even shot them soldiers between the eyes iffin' they was wounded. I ain't never seen white folks do that bad to one another."

"Oh my God, you and your family must have been frozen with fear. I can only imagine what this must have been like for all of you."

In truth I could feel the fear that had permeated the very earth itself. This poor man was vividly reliving the savagery he had experienced.

This big man sits shaking his head and then he puts his head in his hands. The enormity of the moment seems to be poignantly real for him. He is finally able to tell someone what happened and there is a certain sense of relief in telling the story, brutal as it is. I watch him try to regain his composure. The poor man by now has tears streaming down his tragic face. The sheer horror of watching people be murdered in front of you is a traumatic act that no soul can simply 'get over.' I was pretty sure that combining that with how bad his own death must have been, made for severe physical/spiritual trauma. I signaled to the angels to come and to stand by this family and the dead Union soldiers I could see in the background. I had the angels wrap beautiful, glowing, healing blankets around each soul patiently waiting there. I wanted this man to have the opportunity to finish his story, to get it all out, since he seemed to be the spokesman for the whole group. That alone facilitates healing.

"Lady, I was so 'afeared when I heard dem Rebs

comin' in and watchin' all dem Yankees dying in fronta' us that we knowed we was gonna' be dead too, real quick. I felt real bad knowin' what was a comin' for my woman and boy, 'specially my woman. White men folks, does bad things to slave girls, bad things."

The memory of what was still fresh in his mind – since time didn't exist for him – was an unending, recurring, gruesome, trauma.

"Dem Rebs rightly figured we was run-aways, and they sure didn't show no mercy to us. We was so scared we couldn't talk, an it wouldn't have mattered no how. Before I knowd it, that lieutenant says he ain't gonna waste no bullets on slaves, so he has ropes strung up on that big ole oak tree and he hangs us all. They had no mercy for my boy. I guess that hurt the most, the boy was so scared I remember as they slapped the horse out from under me the last thing I saw was my boy's big eyes lookin' at me in cold fear.

"Light Lady, why folks gots to be so mean? Why? We jus' wanted to live like other folks. I been dyin' inside all this time knowin' I couldn' protect my woman and my boy. I couldn' fight that big a Reb group. Damn. If dem' Yankees couldn' do it, what could I do? What could I do?"

"There was nothing you could have done to have prevented this. Every person has a desire to be free and you're no different. You thought you were helping your family to find peace but there are people who don't want peace, they only want power over others. The Civil War was supposed to free the slaves, but the carnage of the process is not something that people can ever understand."

"I reckon you's right. I's just so tired now. So tired. I wanna go home. Is that what you's here to do? Help us to go home? I reckon we's ready to go now."

He looks at all of the soldiers, his wife and son. He is spent. It's time for the war to be over for all of them. I could only imagine the chronic emotional pain he must have suffered every time he looked at his wife and son with that noose around their necks. It was also as if the battle and their murder kept replaying over and over. Sometimes it takes outside intervention to stop such terrible recurring trauma.

The angels assisted all of the soldiers and this slave family. As the souls began to feel nourished by their individual healing blankets, they felt the subtle life force of the divine penetrate their battered souls. I asked that they all be taken to healing stations in the Heaven World so that their mortal wounds could be healed. Those mortal wounds are so profound that they have a devastating impact on the soul. When you ask for healing for those injuries, you can truly offer the soul a special kind of healing: the care, blessing and grace that begin to offer the soul a path into the light. It is a most compassionate act, and the angels are the purveyors of this healing energy.

Finally, as this war weary man ends the line of the dead crossing over, he turns and looks back on that devastating scene as it slowly vanishes. He nods in my direction and slips into the brilliance of the light. I wondered as I watched him walk into that astonishing glow if he realized that he and his family were finally free.

Epilogue

I was glad that this soul was finally able to voice what had happened to all of them. He needed to have history told so that people could understand how costly the Civil War was for so many lives, both soldier and slave alike. Death does not know which side you are on, Rebel or Yankee, and death, the great equalizer, does not know prejudice.

The energy of that entire modern-day neighborhood would have been negatively impacted by this grisly stack of time. Healing this not only helps the living and the dead, but it also helps the earth as well.

When I originally spoke to the modern-day couple, I got the impression that there was a very religious part of them that did not want to accept the concept of a haunted house or location. Yet, they wanted help. Help was provided. However, after their home was cleared, and peace began to reign in their life, they decided that they had only imagined the sounds that had prompted their request for a house clearing. They then denied that there had ever been any sounds or negative sensations there in the first place.

Sometimes denial is an easy access door from the reality of the spiritual realm. Whether or not they choose to believe what happened here, does not deny the positive karma that is created by the service that was rendered to all of those souls.

Terror in 1939

When a United States Air Force couple moved into a relatively new townhouse outside of Ramstein, Germany in the village of Obermohr, they immediately sensed that something was very wrong. Their cats seemed to stare at something, although nothing appeared to be there. The cats, a pair of Lynx Point Siamese seemed to be constantly terrified, exhibiting fearful behavior, actions that they had never displayed before.

Fortunately, their owners were also pretty sensitive to their cats and did not dismiss their actions. They took it seriously when they observed both cats hiding under the covers and looking over their shoulders; their cats were clearly in some kind of emotional distress - but from what? What could their cats see that they, the owners could not? The couple suspected that their cats were seeing a ghost – but who was it?

Considering that they were living in Germany, a country that has been the site of many hundreds of battles in the last century, the couple decided that this could be a very uncertain situation and requested assistance. Here is the story that eventually came from the remote view of their German home.

Through Such Sad Mists of Time

As I began the remote view of their house, I slipped back through the mists or stacks of time, located the property and the time frame in which this ghost was stuck. I had no sooner arrived at the location and begun to look around when a man approached me. I realized from his reaction to me that he seemed to welcome my arrival. It was almost as if he understood why I was there and that he was finally going to receive help. I always find it interesting that when you work in the 4th dimension, you can understand these ghosts no matter what language they originally spoke.

I asked him if he could see the cats in my time period. He had no idea what I was talking about. For him, time was frozen. I asked him his name and why he was still there. He told me his name was Isaac. I think he missed the 'still there' part and simply began to justify his presence. I suspected that there must have been some guilt attached to his presence there; guilt will always cause any soul to linger in the 4th dimension. Isaac desperately wanted me to understand the reason for his actions. Keep in mind that I didn't know what he had done, or why anything he did would have engendered guilt of any kind.

"You have to understand I was so worried about my family! I had to get them out. Things were going badly so quickly that I couldn't allow them to stay. The

Terror In 1939

handwriting was on the wall: the Nazis hated Jews and they were going to kill us all. Rumors were flying around that people were disappearing and no one knew where they went, or what had happened to them. Some of our friends were called out into the street and shot for no reason. There was so much fear surrounding us that we felt sick to our stomachs all the time. I saw men lined up and murdered in the back allies of our town. I had no idea what they had done to be killed like that. We weren't allowed to have more than one person at a time visit us because you could be shot for that as well. One neighbor tried to get people together to talk about what was happening and all of his visitors were shot to death the next day. The Nazi's watched us all the time. We felt like animals in a cage, never knowing when our jailers would decide to kill us, or our children. The Nazis had no mercy on children. I was terrified for my family.

"How would I do it? How would I be able to get them out? Would I ever be able to join them? Where would they go? We were terrified all the time. Why wasn't the world helping us? Didn't they know of our plight? I had to get my family out. I found myself obsessed with this frantic feeling of death coming to us. I couldn't sleep. The less sleep I got, the more my fear seemed to grow.

"My cousin agreed with me that we had to get our families out of Germany at all costs. We had struggled to live in this little village of Obermohr. But this could not continue, so my cousin found a man who was willing to take my wife and children and my cousin's family to Switzerland and perhaps on to either America or to South America, or perhaps Canada.

Ghost Stories from the Ghosts' Point of View

They were to let me know where they were when they arrived, if they could. At least they would be safe there. Somehow, I would find a way to join them. My sincerest hope was that we would all survive the war.

"You have to understand my desperation! We were anxious all the time. We knew that any minute could be our last. Please understand: I did the best I could. I tried my best to protect my family."

I had the distinct feeling that he was trying to convince me that the actions he had taken were the right ones. I felt somehow that he was guilty that he didn't do more for his family. I assured him that I did understand and that I was not there to judge him, I wasn't there to hold any prejudice of any kind against him. My job was only to assist him to cross over. However, it was apparent that he simply wasn't ready. He desperately wanted someone to know what happened to him, to understand his actions.

"Of course, I have great respect for your position at that time. I'm astounded at your courage merely surviving every day. Please, Isaac, it's all right. Take your time. Tell me what happened."

"My family left. My cousin 'took them shopping' in Frankfurt. The Nazis let them go since they had only the clothes on their backs and no luggage. I gave them as much money as I could put together. My small little children cried to leave me, and our sweet little cats. From Frankfurt my cousin was to help them to board a train for Switzerland and then perhaps slip into Italy and then take a boat from there. I had to act as if nothing was wrong, making preparations for their 'return.' I wanted to run with them, I ached to be with them, but I - I had to be patient. If the Nazis thought

Terror In 1939

my family wasn't coming back, if they thought we were all leaving, then none of us would have been able to leave. I had to sacrifice for my family by staying behind when they left.

"You have to know that I prayed every day for my family, that they were safe and yet act as if they were still in my house. I had to pretend as if nothing were out of the ordinary. But I knew I could not keep up the charade forever. The Nazis watched everything and everyone. It was horrible. I knew my days were numbered.

"My family had been gone a month when the Nazis came. They pounded, screaming obscenities at me through the door. I took my time answering them and then as I opened the door, they burst in and started to beat me, wanting to know where my family was. I said they were visiting friends. They beat me harder. I knew I was going to die and would never see my family again. They dragged me out to the front steps of our small home for the entire world to see my final moments, perhaps a lesson to anyone else, who thought they wanted to flee their cruelty. Finally, the most vicious soldier took out his pistol and shot me in the head. As I lay crumpled on the steps, bleeding, I left my body. Finally, I was in a place where the Nazis couldn't find me. I saw a light, but I couldn't leave here, because I must warn anyone else who would live here that it's not safe.

"After I left my body, I followed the Nazis back into my house where they proceeded to ransack the place. We had so little, all the precious things that make life meaningful were shattered, the pictures of my family, the only two that I had were crumpled.

Every single piece of china, handed down from my parents was destroyed. Shattered, like my entire life. At least I still have the memories of my family, the love we all shared.

"My poor terrified cats were hiding and hissing at the soldiers. As the Nazis came closer, they grabbed them, and calling them devil Jew cats, strangled them to death. Then the Nazis stole everything of value that we had ever had.

"I want to leave here. I want to be free of the Nazis, but I'm afraid that God will not be pleased with me that I may have put my family in jeopardy. I did the best I could for them. I keep going over my choices again and again and I don't know what else I could have done. I still need to warn people about this place. Please help me, and my poor kitties. We, my kitties, and I, try to warn everyone not to live here because it isn't safe!

"Now I see these dark 'things' flying around this house. I don't understand this. I have no idea what they are, but they terrify me. Did they come with the Nazis? Are the Nazis a new form of evil on the Earth never seen before? I thought that once I died, I wouldn't be afraid anymore, but there is still the same level of fear in death that I had in life.

"I stay outside because those horrible devil things are inside. The cats go into the house now and then, otherwise they stay with me. I never thought I would still be afraid of this profound evil, even in death. Will I ever be free?"

"Sir, the war has been over for seventy years. You are safe now, you and your sweet cats. Do you see that beautiful angel standing there? He's going to escort all of you to that wonderful light. Once there, you will be able to finally learn what happened to your family. I do not know what happened to them, but you will learn of their whereabouts, soon enough."

I nod to the Angel of Transition waiting to help this man and his cats, that it is time to take them to the crossover point.

"Lady of Light, you can actually see me! Maybe I can be free now. Oh, I can see that there is a light! Is it possible they are coming for me? Is it possible that my torture can finally end? Is that why you're really here?"

"Yes, I've come to help you make this well-earned transition into the light. I know that someone familiar will greet you. Take heart, things will be better for all of you."

"There are beautiful beings coming for me, and they are also taking my precious cats into the light!" He exclaimed through happy tears.

"Now perhaps I will get to know what has happened to my family. Finally, I can be free of this place and the Nazis. Thank you! May God bless you for your kindness!"

Epilogue

Isaac was a good man. He sacrificed himself for the safety of his family, taking a huge risk in the process. Even to this day, we don't know if his family ever escaped. Even though he loved them so much, he was also plagued with guilt that he may have put his family members in jeopardy by sending them away. I think he knew deep in his heart that if they stayed with him, they would be killed. However, he could not have lived with himself had he not tried. His love of others was so great, that even though he could have moved into the light, two things stopped him: one was his concern that God would not be pleased with him because he did not do enough to protect his family, which created his sense of guilt; and secondly, his was concerned for whoever would live in this place even though he did not know that time had passed, and that the war had ended. He felt that he had to warn anyone else who would live in that house that it was not safe.

His cats died a violent death and remained with him as ghosts. These ghost cats and the devilish flying wraiths or dark beings, (that were all over the house, albeit in another dimension) were quite visible to the Air Force couple's pair of Siamese. The cats were terrified of the wraiths and could hear the dead cats hissing and crying.

Once the house was fully cleared, the cats no longer hid and acted in a terrified manner. Their behavior changed by the following day. This told our modern-day couple that all the ghosts and wraiths had been safely removed. This is a very peaceful house now.

There is one more point to make and that is that predecessor energy is not wiped out when a building is destroyed. All the buildings in this housing area are relatively new, not the original buildings standing during the time of the Nazis. Just because you have a new building, there is no guarantee that predecessor energy will not be a challenging problem. In this case, asking the ghost to leave would have been of little value. The stack of time he was in precluded his hearing anyone else's conversation but his own.

The final irony in this case would seem to be the valiant efforts Isaac made to save his family and his apparent dedication to doing all in his power to save others. Despite the extreme prejudice that he endured, he did not become vengeful or prejudiced himself. His sole focus was love and caring, surely these are 'other worldly traits' which make him more than worthy of God's most loving light and protection.

Terror in 1939

Bertha Sue

Did you ever meet a woman who is so brash, so over the top and so powerful that you feel yourself shying away from her?

Did you ever wonder what happens to her after she dies when in life, she had that vengeful sense of entitlement and jealousy?

Did you ever visit a location and notice that, on a subtle level, you can sense a weird, eerie feeling that tells you that something happened here?

Imagine what it would be like to then live in a place where that powerful energy is still operating. You can feel it. You know it's there, but you can't quite put your finger on what it is.

It starts out slowly unnerving you, undermining things in your life, coming at you in the sleep state.

But wait. I'm getting ahead of myself. Let me share this story.

The New Condo

"Hi Tina, I figured I'd better call you to see if you can clear our new place. My boyfriend and I just found this neat apartment not far from downtown Hollywood, and we're really enjoying it. The building isn't new, but the location is great, and they have refurbished each unit."

"How long have you been there?"

"We moved in about a month ago. We've fixed it up so that it's really nice and when we got here, we were pretty happy. But the longer we live here, the more we seem to be fighting about – well nothing really. I can't figure it out. My boyfriend John, is such a good guy and we've always gotten along so well before but man, since we moved here there's been nothing but petty bickering."

Kelly and John are a great couple. They always seemed to be so at peace with each other, so this was out of character for both of them. It felt as if they had fallen out of resonance with each other, or maybe it wasn't with each other. Maybe something else was at work.

"What made you decide to call me? Is there something specific that you've noticed?"

"Well, John seemed to notice it first. He accused me of never turning out the lights when I leave a room. He started a rant about the power bill and how we were spending way too much on electricity and that it was my fault. I must have had a blank look on my face because he got even madder. I was finally able to tell him that I have been turning out the lights in each room. He seemed to think I was being defensive, but I wasn't. I really had turned out the lights.

"Then I found myself becoming increasingly suspicious of him, as if he was not being true to me. He denied it and, of course, this caused a huge fight. Then he got mad at me because he said the house always feels dirty. That was a low blow. I mean we seemed to argue about this for hours."

"Did either of you get sick or have problems sleeping?"

"Yeah, we did, both of us. So far neither of us has had a decent night's sleep since we moved in. It's so bad I'm beginning to think we'll have to move out in order to feel normal again, but it's expensive to move. Oh, and the cough, I keep having this endless tickle in my throat and it never goes away. John has it too, but not as bad. Things are getting worse and worse and I'm feeling so foggy, like I can't concentrate and then I realized that I wasn't getting any acting parts at all. I stopped getting those bit parts that have kept me going."

"Did John have job or financial issues happen?"

"Yeah, we're going through money like crazy and he's beginning to find fault with his job too and that isn't normal for him. He loves his work."

"What caused you to think it might be something supernatural? What caused you to think of me?"

"I got away for twenty-four hours and spent the night with a friend so John and I could have some space in our togetherness. Then it dawned on me when I could think straight that what John and I were experiencing wasn't normal and maybe if we talked to you, we could figure it out."

"So, do you want me to take a look around and get back to you? Has John signed off on this as well?"

"Yes, I explained you to John and he suggested I call you because he agreed that what's been happening isn't normal for either of us. How soon can you start?"

"I can start right away. I'll get back to you."

A Very Occupied Space

Sometimes predecessor energy can be so dark that it can appear as clouds of dark soot. And this is what I discovered as soon as I 'arrived' at their apartment. Mortal people end up breathing in this black, sticky, psychic fog. This negative energy is what makes them cough. That psychic cough is an unproductive, nagging throat tickle. It can start for no reason and it's as if for a few brief minutes, you can't breathe. So, the first order of business was to remove all of this black fogginess. That much psychic soot also makes a home impossible to keep clean. The key is to find the point of origin, the cause of this dark, grungy, negative energy.

As I began to have all of this darkness removed from their home, I realized that the source of the soot was the back bedroom. This room had an energy overlay on it. This means that the energy in that room was coming from the energy of a previous, more powerful building. The longer I scanned this apartment, the more the current spaces vanished, and the dominating origin of the predecessor energy became apparent. Slowly, the original building became visible. Roughly 150 years ago, around 1855-1860, this building was a type of two-story, honky-tonk saloon. It was the kind of sleazy place that cowboys would frequent, belly up to a bar and perhaps find solace in the welcoming ladies who lived upstairs. This would be the place to avoid on a Friday night when men who were way too drunk might become abusive to the pretty, painted women. Bad things could happen during these times.

These ladies of the night would routinely seek a champion for their own entertainment to put off having to accommodate drunken cowboys upstairs. As I was standing there taking in the scene, a big woman dressed in lacy layers that not so discreetly covered her ample chest walked up to me. She wore blood red lipstick, a comical patch of red on each cheek and her hair was a flaming red color. She may have appeared to be the stereotypical 'painted lady,' but she was all business when she opened her mouth.

"Who are ya', honey, and whatcha' doin' in my saloon? Who said you could come in here? I don't allow no church women in my establishment."

"How lovely that you can see me. What's your name?"

"How 'lovely' that I can see you? Get out! I'm Bertha Sue Scott, and I run this place. And no preachy woman's gonna' come in an mess up what I got. Now git!"

She would have looked comical if she were not so physically imposing. She had to be six feet tall and weighed in at well over 200 pounds. Her frilly, sexually inviting clothes seemed oddly out of place on her huge, intimidating almost masculine body. She had enormous hands and the dominating power she wielded over men and women was formidable.

"Well Miss Bertha Sue, I'm not from any church but I am here to help you although perhaps you don't realize what your situation is exactly."

"My 'situation'? Honey, I ain't got no situation, I gots' me a bar and girls to keep my cowboys happy. So, you just git on outta here, you hear, before somethin' bad happens to you!"

"Miss Bertha, do you realize that you are dead and that there is no bar anymore?"

"I ain't dead! I'm talking to ya ain't I? Now git!"

Bertha Sue obviously owned the bar. This woman had to be at least forty years old, but she looked older. Time in those days was not kind to women. As I am getting to know her, I hear a pitiful whimpering somewhere in the background. I can just barely look past her to see another figure, a man with a chest full of bullet holes, frozen with fear in the corner of what must have been an upstairs room that had housed these women and this man.

"Tell me, Madam, who is that man whimpering and cowering in the corner over there? He looks dead to me. Do you know how his chest got to be full of bullet holes?"

"Do I know how his chest got to be full a bullet holes? Yeah, I know exactly how his chest got to be full of bullet holes, causin' I put them holes in his sorry body! Caught the bastard cheatin' on me with one of my girls! He's mine, he wasn't supposed to use my girls. I was the only one he was supposed to have been with. He was MY man, not nary nobody else's! So, I done killed him and left his worthless body in the corner there as a lesson."

"A lesson for who, Bertha? Who else would cross you? And by the way, you do realize that you're as dead as he is, don't you? I mean how else could you see and hear a dead man moaning?"

"I ain't dead! How could I be, I'm a talking to you ain't I, girlie?"

"Bertha, think about it: who killed you? How'd you die? You know you're dead. When was the last time

Bertha Sue

you changed your clothes? Really, a woman in your position must have more than one sexy-lookin' dress."

"Dead? You mean I ain't livin' no more? Well damn! I bet I know when it happened, but I didn't think it'd kill me. One of my girls done somethin' stupid: she fell in love with one a them cowboys. Can't do that in this business. She was the same pretty bitch who fell in love with my man over yonder there. I shot him full of bullet holes with her there watchin' me.

"Sometime after that, she had the nerve to tell me she wanted to leave. Said she fell in love with some no-account cowboy with dreams of starting a ranch. She wanted to start a family. Imagine, that broad a mother!

"In this business, you don't go back to church-lady life. She told me she was leavin' me. I told her to forget it. She belongs to me. I made her what she is. She owed me.

"I made sure she understood that nobody tells me what to do, I tell them. How dare she!

"Well, I reckon one night whilst I was asleepin', she done stabbed me. Guess I thought I was okay but you're telling me I didn't make it. Imagine that and I didn't kill her when I found her with my man! So, what you doing here? What'd you want?"

This whole situation would be almost comical if it weren't so cruel in its raw level of brutality. By now, I pretty much have the story and it's time to move on these two people and anyone else who had the misfortune to die in that saloon during that time. Sometimes when you clear one or two ghosts, you can also assist many others who may be on the periphery in this time stack, to also move into the

Heaven World.

The angels looked so out of place, as they each began to 'work the room' by clearing all of these dead players in this sordid life of alcohol and sex, loneliness and jealousy. I couldn't help but wonder how many men died in and around this spot of earth.

"I see what you're doin'. I ain't goin' with that big bright guy over there. I still gots my say so."

"Yes, Bertha Sue, I'm sure you still have your 'say so,' but the reality is: you are going with him. All of you are going to be leaving right now. My 'say so' as you would call it, pretty much trumps yours, in this situation. But I do have to ask you: are you at all sorry for any of the things you did in this life you just left? Are you at all remorseful for the man you killed?"

"Sorry? Why should I be sorry? Livin' and dyin' don't much matter. They all got what they deserved. Hell, maybe I did too. Guess I'm outta here."

And with that, they were all gone. Where, in the vastness of the Heaven World, a character such as Bertha Sue would end up, is anyone's guess, but at this point she was no longer haunting this apartment building or my clients.

Epilogue

After I removed all the dead I could find in that area, I focused on cleaning up the earth. A saloon brings with it all kinds of negative energy and that feeling will continue to permeate the entire area for several hundred years. Eventually that two-story saloon building was destroyed and possibly more than one building was erected on that spot before the current apartment building was created.

I called Kelly the next day after all the cleaning and clearing was done. I explained the effect of the predecessor energy on her place and the entire building. Cleaning this up will help all the tenants.

"I also wanted you to understand that Bertha wouldn't allow any relationship to exist except what she approved of and if she didn't approve, she would destroy/kill anyone else's relationship. She was determined to control every aspect of the lives of her 'girls' and how they related to the 'johns.' She controlled the energy in this area from her stack of time and that energy was violent, and jealous. When you live in this kind of energy, it would be almost impossible to have any meaningful relationship.

"Now that this is cleaned up, how are you and John feeling?"

"We're feeling so much better! We stopped arguing almost immediately and we can now hear what the other person is saying, oh, and my cough has completely ceased. No doctor I visited could figure out what was causing it. Now I know. This is great, is there anything else that I can do to help the situation?"

"Yes, be sure to do a thorough cleaning of your home, play beautiful music, bring in plants and flowers and spray the entire place with Sweet Orange Oil to cleanse and clear the atmosphere. And be happy. You have probably helped your neighbors far more than you know!"

Bertha Sue

Such an Incredible Stench

"Hi Tina, my name is Bethany Jacobs, here in Virginia Beach. Your sister said I could call you. She said you could maybe help us with this, um, rather embarrassing problem we have in our house. We kinda' think it's a psychic problem? We're not sure. If something doesn't happen soon, we're going to have to sell this house that we just bought not even two months ago."

"I'll be glad to give it a shot. I'm really curious about what's happening on a psychic level that's embarrassing. I'm also guessing that you didn't notice this embarrassing problem when you were looking at the house.

"No! That's the thing. When we looked at this charming cottage here at the beach, we didn't notice anything. It all seemed fine. I mean we walked through every room and there was nothing. Now, oh my God, it's awful and it seems to be growing worse."

"What seems to be 'growing worse?' Oh, and is whatever this is, is it confined to a specific room or area?"

"Yes, it comes almost every single time I'm trying to prepare a meal in the kitchen. It comes when we're watching TV, when we're going to bed. Oh, and it's happened in the middle of the night too. We wake up to this god-awful smell. It comes and goes with no rhyme or reason. It's this sickening stench, that incredible stomach-turning stench!"

Dear Sarah

Once I found the house in time and space, I scanned it and noticed that the house itself (aside from having quite a bit of darkness from several angry teenagers currently living there) was filled with an evil feeling. The teens were bringing in the usual large amount of psychic soot from violent video games and movies. There was already a most oppressive air in the house. When current residents bring in darkness, it is often difficult to separate what they are creating from what was already there from another time and place.

When I began the remote view, I sifted through various stacks of time, but in this case, I didn't have to go back very far. It appeared that the operating stack of time was somewhere in the mid 1950s. When you search for a psychic smell, you have quite a bit of difficulty because normally (if you can ever call this ability normal) you don't smell a location, you only see and get a sense of it, so finding any smell, odor, or fragrance is challenging. However, I wasn't long on this search when I encountered a little girl in the basement of this house. Once I met her, I had a feeling she could help me. She could see me

Such an Incredible Stench

immediately and she spoke to me hurriedly before I could even acknowledge her.

"Hi, my name's Sarah. Have you come to help us? We don't know where to go. You cast such a pretty light and we're so alone and afraid of the dark things coming at us."

Before I could even answer her, say another word, or even introduce myself, she blurted out the situation of this house.

"You got to believe me; we didn't understand that we couldn't eat the food. We were so hungry that we just ate it. Mommy said that it was good for us. I didn't know! I should have protected them! I believed Mommy!"

"Sarah, it's okay, no one's mad at you, I'm not mad at you, I have simply come to help you and to learn about the smell in this house. I just want to understand what happened here. It's okay to tell me. I'm listening."

Sarah seemed to be blaming herself for what had happened. Although just exactly what had happened, I wasn't sure. Sarah began to speak rapidly, nervously, as if she had to hurry to get all the information out or - or something would happen.

"I began to worry about baby John, who I'm guessin's about nine months old 'cause each time he had a bottle, he would throw up, over, and over. Mommy said that he was just sickly and that was the reason that he cried and cried. I watched his face. After each bottle he would act like he was hurtin' real bad inside. Then one night he just died. I went into his bedroom in the morning and found him there. His little body was so cold. I was so afraid. I cried and cried. I went to get Mommy and she picked him up and started crying."

As I am listening to Sarah tell me this story, I am astounded that she found her dead brother. That alone would be traumatic. At this point I am suspecting that Sarah is about five years old.

"The big white and red truck came, and the men said that baby John was a 'crib death' and they were so sorry for Mommy. Daddy didn't talk about it. We didn't get to go to baby John's funeral. I didn't understand what a crib death was, but I didn't think the crib made him die. I wondered if it was his bottle.

"I could still see baby John in his crib, even though they took his body away. So, I telled him he could stay with me. I didn't understand why I could see him and still hear him, but I could. He said he was out of pain now but that he didn't know where he was to go or what to do next. I tried to comfort him. I kept wishin' I had taken that bottle away from him. If only I had warned Mommy that the bottle was making baby John sick, maybe he wouldn't have died. That's what I thought, but it got worse after he died."

In the meantime, as I looked around, I could see four children, 3 very little boys and Sarah who desperately needed love and compassion. Blessedly, as the angels came in, they swooped up the three younger children, wrapped them in blankets of healing and comfort and sat down in rocking chairs and rocked each child right then and there. Finally, when each little boy looked up, he could see a sweet loving face smiling back at him. Then I turned back to Sarah.

"What got worse Sarah?"

"I was real afraid for my other little brothers Jessie

Such an Incredible Stench

and James. My little brother Jesse was two and runnin' all around and then he began to throw up after we would have lunch. James and I looked at each other and were so afeared for Jesse. Sometimes he ate the food and he was ok, and other times, he threw up and his face would look like baby John when he was in all that pain.

"I don't know how to guess time, but Jesse didn't die quick like. It seemed like he took many days to die. His eyes looked black, and he was cryin' all the time. James and I were okay, but Jesse was gettin' worse and worse. He was hurtin' a lot when he tried to go to sleep at night. Doesn't Mommy know that the food is bad? Doesn't she know that the food is hurting Jesse?

"One night during dinner, Jesse fell over in his highchair and I just knew he died. Mommy was cryin' and Daddy didn't say nothin'. He called the white and red truck again, and they took little Jesse away. We never saw him again either. Mommy cried all the time. People came to the house to make Mommy feel better. They didn't know that the food was bad in our house.

"No one came to make me, and James feel better. We cried at night huggin' each other.

"Our house is so sad. James and I are worried that maybe Mommy would get sick and leave us. We was so afraid. We began to be afeared of the food too and tried not to eat, but Mommy said that it wasn't the food that killed baby John and Jesse; it was somethin' else. So, James and I ate the food.

"I got to feelin' sick before James even though I'm a big girl of five. James' only four. My tummy hurt real bad and I told Daddy that the food was bad, but he said he ate the same thing, and it was fine. I didn't want to eat the food no more, but Mommy said I wouldn't get better if I didn't eat something. Soon, I was lookin' like Jesse. Then, James' tummy started hurtin'. Mommy never took us to the doctor, she said that we were fine, and we'd get better soon if we ate what she made for us.

"I remember wantin' the pain to stop so bad and then all of a sudden, I was standing by my body. I guess I died 'cause I could see baby John and Jesse. They said that they could see Mommy puttin' something in the food. We tried to warn James not to eat the food, but he kept eatin' it and then he could see us too. We're all together now.

"I gots all the babies and it's hard takin' care of all of these little boys. I tries real hard, but we don't know where we are or where to go, we just know that if you eat the food in our house, you'll maybe die. We never saw Mommy put stuff in Daddy's food. How come Daddy was okay? We don't know why Mommy put something in the food. Maybe mommies do that.

"Mommy and Daddy went away after James died. We watched new people come to the house. They had kids too. We made a smell, the smell our throw up used to make, to warn them to stay away from here and not to eat the food. We tried to help.

"Is this a bad house? We see all of these little scary monsters running all around us here. What are they? Why are they here? Is there a place we can go to, to be safe from the bad food? I don't know if I'll ever be able to eat again."

She looked down at where her feet would be.

Such an Incredible Stench

Even though there was an angel next to her, she seemed blinded by her fear and the weight of her responsibility for her brothers. I could readily feel how powerless she must have been in the days and weeks that she watched all of her brothers die those agonizing deaths. Her own death made her feel powerless. She must have watched in abject horror as her mother cried over the demise of each child, while at the same time she was systematically poisoning them all to death.

Finally, when it appeared that Sarah had told me all that she could, all that was on her mind, she suddenly seemed to notice the beautiful angels rocking her brothers.

"Oh, Light Lady, look at all of these pretty angels! They're here to help us, right? Are they takin' us to that bright light?"

This was the first time I could see any hope or light in Sarah's young face. The agony of watching her siblings die one by one had left Sarah in a perpetual state of grief and fear. Now, at last, she seemed to brighten. I said a silent prayer that Beings of Light come to greet each child and welcome them home, since I was not sure if there would be family members there to greet them. I wanted to make Sarah and her brothers feel absolutely safe. She was going to need to learn how to trust again and this transition to the Heaven World would be an important first step.

As Sarah turned to follow her siblings into the Heaven World, I heard her talking to her angel escort.

"Maybe we'll be okay now. Oh, beautiful angel, please tell the Light Lady thank you."

Epilogue

Little five-year old Sarah was carrying a terrible responsibility: warning people of the possibility that death loomed in this house. She was also terrified of the little monsters that she saw in her 4th dimensional world. These creatures were Lower Realm Intelligences, basically, called forth from the darkness created by the murderous mother. Once any violent act or murder has taken place, a profound darkness will descend on that home. This darkness has a grimy, filthy quality to it, almost the consistency of damp soot. With each additional heinous deed, the darkness increased. The 3 foot-high, spindly, inky black monsters, or Lower Realm Intelligences literally came from a dark hole created by the negativity of that method of death. But what caused Sarah's mom to kill all of her children?

It is possible that the mother had Munchausen's by Proxy Syndrome. This is a mental disorder whereby the mother slowly sickens her child and then basks in the sympathy of friends and family as a child endures a prolonged hospital stay and endless tests, or repeated visits to emergency rooms. In severe situations the mother perpetrates the death of her children as in this case. Whether or not the authorities ever figured out that the mother was the cause of the deaths of all of these children, we will never know.

What makes this story especially heartbreaking is that neither Sarah nor her younger brothers knew what to do at death and this situation is not uncommon. Children look to adults to guide them, but if they are murdered, or die in a tremendous tragedy, there is no one they recognize who can lead them. It

Such an Incredible Stench

is important to remember that anyone can ask for angels to guide ghost children to the light.

Once Sarah and her brothers were provided angels, and assisted into the Heaven World, then the Lower Realm Intelligences were also removed.

And finally, once all of this was done, that incredible stench, finally disappeared.

I asked that the current homeowners send prayers to all of these children. Angelic assistance and prayers of healing and compassion help all souls, no matter how long ago they may have died.

Such an Incredible Stench

Her Punishment

So many times death does not bring relief, release or reflection. Often, death brings on an almost murderous rage to the soul who now finds that he or she has trapped themselves in a hell of their own making. The unsettling facet to this rage is that it can echo out into our dimension, into our own mortal reality with chilling consequences. The energy of this anger is what creates the paranormal anomalies that incite fear in even the most courageous of us.

This case takes us into the realm of that tragic angry place, that place where you have to truly listen before you can help someone. Peace can only come after the person can share his or her story.

The Frantic Call

Late one afternoon I received a frantic call from a close friend. She was at home with her husband, their son and their housekeeper and she begged me to come over immediately. When I inquired as to what was wrong, she said that someone, or something utterly unknown was haunting their house and I had to come and 'fix it RIGHT NOW!'

Ghost Stories from the Ghosts' Point of View

"Wow okay, I'll be right over." I told her.

Funny how sometimes fear can make you feel cold, like you are shivering with cold, but it isn't cold, it's fear, cold fear even on a very hot day. The scene I encountered when I let myself in through the open front door was that chill in the air of the family's overwhelming terror.

I was a bit astonished to find all four of them huddled in a corner of the living room watching the center of the room. These are highly educated people, and while they do believe in ghosts, they never expected to actually have one in their home. It's one thing to realize your home may be suddenly haunted, it is much more unnerving to witness this ghost or ghosts tossing small objects through the air, like CD cases, or moving paintings. This family even felt this ghost whooshing past them with such intensity that they could feel some semblance of a ghost body brush against their bodies. It goes beyond having the hair stand up all over you. The chilling facet of facing a real paranormal nightmare in broad daylight invokes a profound feeling of helplessness and dread.

And they all felt it. They all knew they were not collectively crazy. They told me that within the last couple of days, they had each begun to sense that someone was there, but it wasn't too bad. What often happens is that when one person senses a ghost, so does another family member but neither of them mentions it to anyone else. Each person tries to dismiss it as just an anomaly, something that will 'pass in time' or 'just go away.'

But when it doesn't pass or go away, you come

face to face with the fact that there's something going on. And that is exactly what happened.

I asked them when they began to notice 'something.' For each person it was a bit different. For the parents and the housekeeper, it was just a little 'something' out of the corner of their eye, a sense of unease, a feeling that someone was there but then each person wasn't quite sure of it. The vagueness of it allowed them to ignore it until their son arrived.

Once their son, Sean, came over to spend the evening with his dad and his dad's new wife, (he was currently living with his mother,) everything escalated. This was when they could feel the ghost or ghosts rushing past each of them, however, their son seemed to be the focus of all of the heightened psychic activity. The poor guy had no idea why. He just drove over to visit his parents and have a nice evening with them all. He looked at me in a bewildered way and shrugged his shoulders. He was just as puzzled as the rest of them standing there terrified of the unknown, the unseen but that definitely present – something.

By the time I actually arrived at the house, they were now all experiencing ghostly phenomena. The more they described what had been happening the more it felt like someone on the other side was trying to get their attention. I could feel the energy of whoever was there, but I knew I needed to begin working quickly.

A Mountain of Murderous Rage

I was sitting in the living room by myself. Normally,

Ghost Stories from the Ghosts' Point of View

I don't go to the person's house to remove a ghost, but since they were so close and they desperately wanted my presence in the house, I agreed to come over.

As I began to work, the rest of the family was watching from the hallway. I'm not sure what they thought was going to happen, but I guessed that they wanted to keep a 'safe' distance away from what must surely have felt like a mini maelstrom.

As I 'looked' around and got a sense of things, I immediately noticed two elderly people who had followed the husband home from his medical practice. They were pretty benign, and I was able to move them on rather quickly. The third ghost, however, caught me completely by surprise – he body slammed me and then grabbed me by my throat!

And he grabbed me so hard, with such dynamic, terrifying force that I could feel his hands on my throat beginning to crush my windpipe. When you can't breathe, panic immediately begins to set in and all you want to do is to get that person's hands off of your throat so you can feel fresh air fill your lungs. I completely forgot that my purpose was to try to reason with what is obviously a murderous ghost! But he just wouldn't let go of me. I had my own hands on my throat trying to get him to release me as I was struggling to breathe.

The dad was watching me gasp for breath with my hands on my throat. Since he is a physician, he ran for his kit. I realized as I could hear him screaming at me that he was preparing to do a tracheotomy right then and there. Now I'm really shoving sheer blind panic into high gear! I didn't want to die that day myself, but I surely didn't want to have this doctor cut my throat open, either.

Finally, I got a grip on my own emotions and began to talk to this teenage ghost.

"Who are you?" I asked in as calm a voice as I could muster under these dire circumstances. I have never heard a ghost scream at me until this event, but scream, he did.

"Why do you care? NO ONE CARES! There's only hate in the world! I'm ANGRY!! And I don't know who you think you are or why you're here but if you think you can dispatch me as quickly as you did those old people, you're dead wrong! I'm not going ANYWHERE!"

I can feel my friend moving toward me with his scalpel and I realized that I had to take my power back from this vicious ghost and get him to stop. So, I yelled at him with a demanding power in my voice.

"Tell me your name RIGHT NOW and TAKE YOUR HANDS OFF OF ME IMMEDIATELY! You're killing me!" I demanded. Amazingly, that startled him enough that he instantly released me. Blessedly, I could feel his cold, icy hands release my throat and feel the reassuring sensation of life-giving air rush back into my lungs. The wide-eyed doctor put his medical things away when I gave him the signal that I could breathe again. Everyone seemed to give a collective sigh of relief.

Brian's Sad Story

"My name is Brian Schmitt."

"Brian Schmitt, the same Brian Schmitt who

committed suicide about a year ago?

"Yes, I am."

What made my conversation with him so amazing was that I was talking to him out loud in this room. The family could hear my side of the conversation. Once I took charge of the situation, incredibly, he began to calm down. I then asked him to tell me what happened that caused him to kill himself.

"I hate my mom! She was divorcing my dad and it was all her fault! She was the cause of everything! My dad didn't want the divorce, but she went through with it. I watched my dad feel so destroyed and she was to blame. What a bitch!"

"Brian, how old were you?"

"I am seventeen."

He answered me flatly almost emotionless as if he did not realize until that moment that he had thrown away the rest of the life.

The longer I questioned him, the more he seemed to be replacing his rage with profound despair. In a gentle but firm voice, I asked him to tell me what happened on the day he died.

"The divorce was becoming final. I had been on the computer that evening and she came into my room and began screaming at me to get off of it, bitching and moaning that I was on some 'bad' site. I screamed back at her and we had a huge fight. I hated her so much at that moment! Then she had to go out of the house to deal with some other divorce thing. She finally left me alone."

"How long had you planned to kill yourself? When did that thought come to you? There's no judgment here. We all simply want to understand what

Her Punishment

happened inside of you."

Although his response was disturbing, chilling me to my core, he told me the story dispassionately, almost as if he were telling me what he saw someone else do. He seemed disconnected from it all. But gradually, elements of the tragedy, of his experience began to seep into the feeling of his words.

"At that moment, I remember feeling rage, a rage that I guess just exploded and I wanted to punish her for destroying our family. Right after she left the house, I was so angry that I wanted her to feel the pain I was feeling so I decided to kill myself right then. I knew that she would be back pretty soon. Dad wasn't allowed to come to the house. But it was his house too! But she wouldn't let him come here. I planned it so that she would be the one to find me. I decided to hang myself in my bedroom. I knew she would come into my room when she got home, so I hung myself from the ceiling fan. I wanted her to find my body. I wanted her to feel the horror of seeing my lifeless body. That was the only way I could make her understand how mad I was at her."

I took a deep breath and began to digest what this poor kid had just said; I knew that I had to help him to understand his entire situation.

"Once you hung yourself, son, do you remember leaving your body?"

"Yeah, hanging yourself is a horrible way to die. . ."

I continued on.

"Once you left your body, did you watch your mom come in and find you?"

"Yeah, I watched. I didn't expect her to call my

dad, though. That bitch called him and forced him to come over and see my body. I – I forgot how bad my dad would feel when he realized I was dead. I had no idea he would see me hanging there. I didn't mean for that to happen. But it was all her fault! I watched him cry. She screamed for a while and then she called 911. I watched them cut me down from the fan and take my body away. I thought I'd feel better dead, but I don't feel any better dead than when I was alive. I thought that killing myself would take my rage away. Death doesn't take away the anger and the pain. I'm still furious."

"Son, I have to ask you, what is your connection to your friend Sean here?"

"We went to different schools, but we knew each other because our families were friends – until my mother ruined everything. I knew his parents were divorced, too, but that his dad had remarried. I followed him one day and just hung around here watching the crap that was happening to his family. Why do parents fight so much when kids are in high school?"

"I don't know. It's what happens, I guess. Tell me, what was it about today that caused everything to accelerate for you to make such an effort to get everyone's attention?"

"I came . . . I came to try to get him to understand that even though your parents divorced, killing yourself is not the answer."

"Oh my God, did you think that Sean was thinking along the same lines? Did you think Sean was planning on killing himself?" This was truly a rare situation where I could have a conversation with this ghost out loud. I relayed what Brian was saying so that the family could know what was going on between both Brian and me.

Sean is over in the corner shaking his head and telling his family that he was not thinking of killing himself! His dad is staring at him in horror. He takes his dad aside to reassure him that he was not thinking about suicide.

"Well, I didn't know for sure, and I wanted to tell him, but he couldn't hear me, and I felt this rage come up again. I knew he was mad at his parents. I guess killing yourself doesn't really solve anything does it?"

I could sense that Brian was beginning to allow remorse to enter his heart and that he was feeling the profound tragedy of it all. However, I couldn't understand why he attacked me.

"I have to understand why you came at me so violently when I came in to try to help you. What were you thinking when you saw me?"

"I was angry. You looked like you were going to try to stop me from convincing Sean over there not to kill himself."

"Sean had no idea what you were trying to do. You terrified him with your swooping around him and making things fly through the house. Now he knows exactly what you were feeling and that you genuinely wanted to help him." Here again, I was glad that I could share this entire conversation with them out loud.

"I guess you're right. It sucks to be a ghost. No one hears me. The only way I can get anybody's attention is to move stuff around, and that takes a lot of energy. But then I have lots of energy. Rage gives you energy for a while, then it just makes you sad inside."

I sensed that Brian's rage had begun to dissipate and that it was finally time to help him cross over. An angel offered his hand. Brian seemed reluctant to take the bright, welcoming hand that was extended to him.

"It's alright to take the angel's hand. It's time to cross over and begin to heal." He shook his head and looked like he wanted to cry but he was fierce in his refusal to give in to tears.

"It's alright to let go, son. The angel will take you to a place where your broken heart can heal. You'll feel better soon. Do you see that light that's coming for you? Breathe it in. It's all right. You're safe now. Crossing over will help your whole family to heal."

He looked at me with tragedy in his eyes and reluctantly took the angel's hand. Then he was gone.

I opened my eyes and asked everyone if they were all right. The three of them stared at me with shock on their faces. They each said that this was an incredible experience. They were so glad that they could participate in helping him cross over by asking for help. I know that they joined me in my astonishment at this young man's towering rage. I assured them that their request for help is tremendous for Brian and their service to him will echo out for a very long time.

Epilogue

When a person who commits suicide finally crosses over, it greatly enables the living family members to heal. It is a subtle yet significant difference. Eventually I felt that Brian was truly sorry for his extreme decision to end his life. It was my prayer for him, that he received help in the Heaven World to heal all of those aching places in his heart. I also sent prayers to his family to facilitate healing for all of them.

My friends called me later and said that their house was psychically quiet now. Nothing else is flying around, no one was whooshing past them, and they felt 'alone' in their house. They also said that they realized how important it is to work out an agreement between former spouses to remain civil at all times for everyone's sake.

The reality is that an astonishing number of parents tend to divorce each other when their children are in high school. This is the time in a teenager's life when boys and girls need their parents the most. Yet, parents become completely overwhelmed by their own sense of hurt and betrayal and become blind to the catastrophic reaction their behavior is having on their children. Tragically, divorce is love betrayed for children of any age and its emotional consequences echo out for the rest of everyone's lives.

Her Punishment

The Exit Strategy

Sometimes a soul is weary, intensely so.
Sometimes a soul is not totally truthful within itself.
Sometimes a soul simply longs for release.
Sometimes a soul can no longer bear the pain of the burdens of career, family, friends, and the endless obligations.

These feelings are not usually part of a person's conscious awareness. Yet these feelings do operate in a subtle way that sadly causes the soul to quietly seek an exit strategy despite the deep affection of family and friends.

And such is the case in the following story of a much beloved man coming home one chilly night in January on a long windy road in Charleston. This man had been my neighbor many years prior when I had lived in South Carolina.

"This Wasn't How I Planned to End My Day"

"Hi Mark, I'm surprised to see you here. I thought

surely, you'd be with your family tonight." I really was quite surprised to see him standing in my office. He had died the previous week in what, to friends and family, was a senseless accident.

"I've been with them, but the agony and the fury of their grief was more than I could to bear. They're all so mad at me!"

"I'm sure they are. Neither your family, your friends nor your office staff could believe that, at the age of 66, you were still riding a motorcycle."

When I heard the news of his death, I found myself dumbfounded by the senselessness of it. Riding a motorcycle at 66? I had to ask myself what he was thinking.

His colleagues begged him not to ride that bike. His kids and his wife had pleaded with him not to even start with it, but he could never be dissuaded.

What made this death even harder to swallow was that, as an orthopedic surgeon he had spent numerous long hours repairing the bones, hips, and shredded muscles of many an immortal-minded motorcycle rider. It wasn't like he didn't have first-hand experience with the 'casualties of the open road.'

"I know they're angry. I know I made a stupid over-correction. Really, I consider myself an outstanding cycle rider. I'm safe, courteous, wear the right clothes and I'm excellent at anticipating what other drivers are going to do. I do understand how dangerous it is. I ride my bike with a great deal of respect for the dangers, yet I also have a good level of confidence. I've done really well all this time."

". . . until you didn't, until that last move killed you."

The Exit Strategy

Mark got really quiet. Then he continued again, in the present, as if he had not fully absorbed that his conversation about himself should logically have been in the past tense.

"You have to understand, Tina, this wasn't how I planned to end my day. I had plans for that night, that weekend. I mean, going to my own funeral wasn't part of the plan!"

He looked toward his feet and seemed startled to realize that he was no longer grounded, that he no longer touched the earth. He seemed to feel sick as he gazed upon his shredded clothes, now very red with his own blood. Blunt force trauma will do that to you.

"So please tell me what did happen that night."

"Look, I'm a great rider, I follow all the safety rules. I'm mindful of other drivers, but I don't know why that night was so unusual somehow. I've driven up that hill a thousand times and that night wasn't any different. I wasn't even driving that fast. The evening started out great. I went to a soccer match after a full day at the office. I had a great time. Then, it had to be 9:30 pm or so when I headed home. It was a clear night as I cruised up the road. As I was banking on a slight curve, right smack in my path was a skunk.

"Do you realize in all the time that I've been riding that bike I've never, ever crossed paths with a skunk before? It all happened so fast. I remember thinking that if I hit the skunk my bike might slip on his guts, and I'd lay the bike down or go home with a smelly bike. I knew I didn't want that, so I decided to just veer around him. It was so quick. By the time I realized I had to go around him I think I must've actually jerked the bike to avoid the skunk and ended up overcorrecting.

"I didn't realize that I was so close to the curb as I hit it. Next thing I knew, I was flying through the air and landed in a crumpled heap next to a bunch of water pipes. Immediately, I kind of shook off the fall and found myself surprised that I had no pain. I could see my bike and I realized as I walked over to it that it was totaled.

"Then I reached for my cell phone to call my wife, Vicki Sue, but I couldn't get the phone to work. Then a car stopped, and I saw the guy hop out and go over to my body. He was trying to see if I was OK. I think it was then that I realized that I had left my body. I stood there and watched as the paramedics eventually came, as the police took reports and finally it all became a blur of flashing lights, shaking heads, and sad faces.

"The next thing I knew I was standing by my wife. I wasn't sure how I got there. Then I was back by my body as the EMT's worked on me. Then I heard them pronounce me dead at the scene.

"How can I convey the horror of suddenly realizing that I can't return to a dead body, to my own body. I went into a kind of shock I didn't know could exist.

"It's such a horrible feeling. I felt wave after wave of crashing emotions. At one point, I saw my entire life pass before me. Seeing that was both heartening and sad: I've had such a great life! But then I also realized with a sickening feeling how angry everyone would be at me for leaving them, for dying on that bike. . . all because I didn't want to hit that skunk."

"Mark, were you present when they told your

wife?"

"Yeah, I was standing beside her when the police finally came to my house at three in the morning. Vicki Sue wasn't asleep. I think she knew something happened to me and she was just hoping it wasn't serious.

"There is no way to describe the torture of watching as the officer informs your wife of your death. I can't describe her grief, shock, and anger at me. Then she had to call all five of our kids and then my business partner, office staff and close friends. Those same waves of grief, shock, and anger at me just kept coming over and over as each person tried to process the reality of my death. Over and over and over. . . and I felt the emotion of each of them as their initial grief washed over them. It's an indescribable torture. It's so hard.

"I had to listen again and again as each person went numb inside; I thought watching my wife get the news was horrible enough - and it was -but watching each of my kids learn of my death was torture on an entirely new level, like some kind of cruel karma.

"I didn't get to say goodbye to anyone. I didn't get to tell my wife how much I loved her or tell my children how privileged I was to have been their dad. You know you always think you can say goodbye, that you have plenty of time, but you don't.

"It all happened so fast."

"Did you go to your funeral? Were you there? Did you listen as each person talked about your life together?"

"Yeah, I heard them tell me how much they'll miss me and how angry they are that I refused to give up my bike.

"I heard my daughter lament that I won't be there when she graduates from med school, never get to walk her down the aisle or be a grandfather to her children. She was so angry that I wouldn't be there to take care of my little girl. It was devastating!

"My sons were crying. One son sounded like he was in agony. All my boys said they couldn't believe I wouldn't be there for advice and counsel, to share their lives and their families with them. I was well, I – I'm devastated.

"Friend after friend came up and spoke. Some were angry. Some were sad. Some recounted great experiences, happy times we'd had together.

Finally, one of my sons talked about the book about Christ that I read right before the accident. I had given the book to many family members and friends. Jesus talked about life everlasting, that there really is no death. It was at that point that I made that white dove fly into the church, to let them know that it's all true! I'm still here. I left a fragile body but my soul, who I am, is still here, still loves and grieves right along with them. That's what I wanted them to understand, but I think I only scared them. You could've heard a pin drop in the church after the dove flew around and then left.

"You know, when I died, I told you that my whole life passed before my eyes, and I realized that I had a great life. I lived and I loved. I enjoyed being a husband and father. I loved being a surgeon. But having my kids, my wife and my own brothers talk about me at the funeral was harder than the life review. I can also feel that they are all holding on to

The Exit Strategy

me for dear life, as if the thought of my being really gone is unfathomable.

"I keep feeling the impact of the tragedy of that split second decision to avoid that skunk. Imagine the skunk's alive and I'm not. A skunk ended it all."

"I could feel how deeply he was moved by the grief he had unwittingly caused. However, he never once mentioned or even hinted that he regretted riding that motorcycle."

"Mark, as I listen to you feel the pain of all who knew and loved you, I have yet to hear you say whether or not you regret that you were on your bike that night. Had you been in your Corvette, we wouldn't be having this conversation. Are you sorry you rode that bike?"

"No, not really. How do I explain it? How can I convey the exhilarating sense of freedom that I felt on that bike? I was so happy riding it, feeling that I was one with the bike, with nature, with the road.

"Everyone told me it was dangerous. I knew that, yet when I was riding, I savored those moments of freedom: freedom from my practice, from all of the heavy feelings of responsibility that come with my profession. I lived. I really lived.

"I'm sorry and saddened by the pain my family feels but I have to tell you that I'm not sorry for the life I lived. I truly enjoyed this life. I loved being a doctor. I loved my patients, my office staff.

"I was blessed with a wonderful wife – she lit up my life. She made me so happy and, together, we had this great life and fantastic kids.

"I loved being a dad, watching all my kids grow up, participating in their lives. I had it all. I lived it all but it's over now. I get that they're angry though. I get it."

"I was struck by the fact that he wasn't remorseful for swerving his bike that night. He didn't regret living or the way he lived. Obviously, he had an understanding of the risks. He knew he could have survived that night had he been in a car but being thrown from a motorcycle and having your entire body crash into all of those water main pipes on the side of that road wasn't survivable."

I often wonder if the soul unconsciously is ready for death. Mark seemed sad for his family and friends but not necessarily sad that he died.

"Are you upset that you died?"

"A little, but I have no regrets. I've seen what the ravages of age do to people. I knew that I was challenged keeping up with the changing technology of robotics in medicine, not to mention the billing issues and the ever-growing mountain of government regulations. Frankly, it was getting harder and harder to keep up with it all. Between e-mail, all the social things I did, my practice, kids, friends -- it was exhausting. I guess I was more tired than I realized. I watched colleagues have heart attacks, commit slow suicide by alcohol, get sued or have to cut back hours just to keep their sanity.

"I mean, I was keeping up, but I guess in a way I was tired. This isn't a bad way to leave. You know what I'm saying? Am I a bad person because I feel this way?"

He seemed genuinely perplexed. Talking made him realize what he lost and what he had. It also enabled him to see that, perhaps on another level, this was not just a tragic motorcycle accident. It was a quick and virtually instant exit strategy. That concept would be very tough for those who loved him to understand.

"Mark, why are you here with me now? Are you ready to leave?"

"I knew when my friend called you about my death, that you would help me. I do see the light. I just can't seem to get myself to fully enter that place. I never gave any real thought to what happens after death. I thought it would take care of itself, but it doesn't. I know I could linger, could follow my wife around or my kids. I've been doing that since I died. But I can't hear that agony anymore. I've said what goodbyes I can, and I guess it's time to do this thing, whatever that is."

"This angel will guide you home. I'm sure there will be friends and family members to greet you as you make your final crossing. And Mark, you led a wonderful, honorable life."

"Thanks, I knew I couldn't stay, couldn't keep hanging around as a ghost. I mean how weird is that? My family's grief is more than I can continue to bear. I also knew that they would each try to hold me here. They had already begun. The longer I linger, the more powerfully I can feel them clinging to me for dear life. It's time to go."

He turned toward the angel and the growing light.

"I can already feel the peace! Thanks for the help!"

. . . and, with that, he was gone.

Epilogue

Most people never imagine how hard their passing is going to be on their families. Even if a soul is ready to leave on an unconscious level, that person's family is likely not ready at all. However, Mark's transition into the light will ultimately help them to grieve and then be able to let go and move forward with their lives without him.

When you love someone so dearly, you can unconsciously hold that person on the 4th dimensional plane, preventing him or her from crossing over. The more people who hold on to a soul emotionally, the more difficult it is for the soul to ever enter the Heaven World. The soul literally becomes a prisoner of everyone's unintentional grasping hearts. It's easy to understand. You love someone and you don't want to release them, but it is critical to understand that holding the soul here hurts the one who died and isn't really helpful to those who remain.

Fortunately, for all concerned, Mark knew he needed help and he sought it out. That alone is unusual. Most souls have no idea who to ask for help in such a challenging and often heartrending situation. In the end, his transition to the Heaven World was the best for everyone.

Helen Stanton

Assisting the dead is profound service indeed. I found myself deeply impressed by the kindness of the mistress of this property. The owner may not have known exactly what she was dealing with, but she knew that she really needed help, she just didn't realize on how many levels. Sometimes, it is cases like this that remind me how noble the human spirit truly is and how honored I am to be of service in such situations. And so, what began as a simple request to remove a ghost in a condo in Virginia Beach, Virginia became one of my most inspiring encounters.

So Much Work to Do

"What took you so long? I've been waiting for you, for what seems like forever!"

Obviously, she was in a hurry to get this done. Most people who have lived with a ghost for a while are just glad that someone finally shows up who believes in ghosts and can actually help both the ghosts and the homeowner.

"I'm so sorry. I didn't realize that you were waiting for me specifically. I got here as quickly as I could."

"I really didn't know who else could help me with this. Do you?" She was very businesslike.

"Well, I don't know anyone else who does this exactly. I guess I thought that perhaps other people could do this, but no matter, I'm here now and I'm ready to get to work."

"I'm Helen Stanton, and it's nice to meet you. How long did it take you to notice me, or I should say, find my place?"

"Not long. I found my way pretty readily."

She was an imposing woman with an impressive presence. I didn't expect her to be so tall. She was quite plainly dressed but she seemed like such a strong person. I loved the graciousness of her Southern drawl.

"[She sighed] I'm so glad. You know, my roommate has probably known for some time, but I guess it just took her quite a while to figure out that she needed to actually help me with this problem."

"I realize that sometimes people must seem a bit, shall we say, dense to you."

"Dense? Well, darlin' that would be an understatement! People, the ones I can actually connect to, are so uncaring. You know, they know I'm here, but they don't even acknowledge me. It's so insulting and often, well, really, I find it cruel."

She must have felt so alone with her belief in ghosts. That kind of willingness to help the dead can be a very solitary path, and she did seem intent on getting help.

"I know. Whatever happened to that old fashioned sense of courtesy we have always known in the South?" I commented.

"I don't rightly know. The South I know is such a mess right now. It's heart breakin.' This beautiful area that I know and love, is such a disaster! Everyone's so angry! Politics has pitted brother against brother, family against family. Will things 'round here ever settle down? I know that you can see the future, can you please ease my sad heart and tell me if things are ever gonna' get better for my beloved Virginia?"

"Let me assure you, Helen, things will get better. Life will calm down. But from your viewpoint as we talk about this, I can see that it will take a good 140 years for things to fully come to a place where we'll all be at peace, we'll all be looking at each other in a different light."

"I'm so glad to know that there is a brighter future for us all. Right now, it's such a tragic place. I've been so alone, just waiting for things to finally change."

"I am so sorry that you've been so alone, waiting here. You're shivering Helen, are you cold?"

"Cold! I've been so cold for so long, funny that you would ask that. Hopefully, I can finally 'warm up' now that you've come at last."

"Can you help me to understand how you are so aware of just where you are and who you are? You are totally unusual. Most people in your position are utterly clueless regarding their circumstances."

"Perhaps I am unusual. I reckon I've always known from that moment just exactly where I am and what I am now. I'm not under any illusions. And yes, believe me, I've been 'round long enough to know how things work. And yes, I've seen the light!"

"Then, I must ask you, why are you still in the position you're in? Why've you been waiting for me?"

"Because I simply couldn't leave them. They don't understand like I do and without you, I had no way to help them."

"Help who? Helen, who couldn't you leave?"

"Come on outside with me. Look over yonder. Do you see them?"

"Good Lord! There must be at least 200 of them!"

"Exactly! And every one of them needs more help than I can provide them alone. They know I'm tryin' to care for them, and I keep tellin' them that help is 'acoming and now – help is actually, finally, blessedly here! I guess my prayers have finally been answered."

"So, they don't know they are . . .?"

She quickly interrupts me, "No, all them boys have no idea."

"Okay, Helen, then let's get busy."

"Before we get started, though, before I go. Thank you, thank you for coming and being willing to do this."

"You are quite welcome, Helen. It's my profound pleasure to be able to do this for you and for them. I hope that my work here will help you all. But Helen, I must thank you for your truly astonishing service of never leaving these soldiers."

"For these men, and for me, your work is literally 'life changin'.' I have felt desperate for help. I'm seein' more and more men arriving in these woods every day. It was as if they had no place to go. Maybe they felt that something was changin'. I don't know. All I know is that after a while it became almost unbearable to be with them; they're so sad and in so much pain."

"Then let's get started."

"We're all ready."

I couldn't help myself. I was utterly blown away by the goodness and the caring that Helen exhibited. Her loyalty to these men was amazing. I was so impressed by this woman! And now it was time for me to begin my work. My angelic team was standing by. It was time to begin my spiritual prayer.

"Very well. Then I hereby request my team of Angels of Transition to come right now and remove all of these souls to the appropriate realm of the Heaven World. I am requesting a special Archangel to personally escort my heroine, Helen Stanton, to the Heaven World. Truly, her spiritual service has earned her this courtesy. Her stalwart loyalty to all of these mortally wounded Confederate soldiers is service in the highest tradition of the mortal and the spiritual realm. I ask that she receive special healing for her sad heart and the shattering gunshot wounds that fatally shredded her frail body. I also request that all of the soldiers she has so faithfully assisted also receive healing. I thank you, Heavenly Father, for this assistance for all of these ghostly souls."

At this point, Helen is sobbing tears of blessed relief.

"Finally, I can feel the warmth! Finally, I can see that the light I have so longed to join is coming for us all. Night after night I've been whispering in the homeowner's ear to get us some help. Finally, she heard me and called you. Thank you!"

"Thank you, Helen. Today, for all 200 or more wounded souls you have been valiantly caring for, the Civil War is finally over. Now you can all go home to your loved ones, to the Father who has so loved you. Finally, you all are free from the violence that has held you here in that nether world of timelessness on the Earth plane."

As the light embraced Helen, so it also welcomed all of those bewildered soldiers. These men could finally feel the pain of their agonizing wounds leave them. The ones who had no legs could now walk. The ones who had tortuous abdominal wounds felt their bodies restored. The ones who had been filled with guilt for all of the men they had killed, some of them friends and neighbors, could finally be free of that horrible pain of their crisis of conscience. Many soldiers were blind from powder burns; others had hideously infected wounds. All of them were cold and shivering. I could feel them all relax as the pain left them. However, they hesitated, waiting for Helen to assure them that it was okay to go into that benevolent, warming, healing light. She smiled at them all and let them know that it was finally okay to enter that glorious place. She would not cross over herself until the last man was welcomed into the light.

"At last, we are all going home. My job is finally done, and no one is left behind. We are all feelin' the peace of bein' released from the agony of this horrific War Between the States."

I could see how bright her face and body were becoming. I also filled her with my own love and admiration for truly I felt I was in the presence of greatness – of what it means for one soul to sacrifice herself for another.

"Goodbye Helen. May God wrap you in profound love, healing light and divine blessings."

The angels looked back at me with smiles as they escorted her into the light and the scene slipped away. When I looked around the property one last time, it was empty. It felt quiet somehow, as if there had been a great deal of activity and now that was over. The land finally felt peaceful.

"I Guess I Knew She Was Here."

When I explained the details of her ghost to quiet, soft-spoken Shelly, the modern-day homeowner, she seemed most pleased that she had been able to help Helen. She told me that she had long suspected that she had a very kind ghost in the house. She had felt for several months that she needed to have her house looked at, either Feng Shui or something. She felt an urgency to get help from someone for her house. She told me that she was not specifically afraid, but she had that felt 'pressured' to find a psychic.

With Helen actually gone, with the hundreds of Civil War dead no longer haunting the entire property, she found that she was sleeping so much better. She did feel Helen's absence, but she continually sends Helen and the soldiers love, healing, and prayers. We both smile whenever we think of this valiant soul.

One Last Remnant of the Civil War

Once I had finished this job, which took several evenings to process and clear, I asked Shelly to let me know how things were going over the next several days. She called me back about a week later, surprised: now she keeps smelling sage. I agreed to check this house one more time to make sure I had located all of the ghosts that were influencing this piece of property. It was then that I stumbled upon another aspect of that unique Civil War stack of time.

I was not quite sure he even realized he was dead. He was so intent on his task. I had no idea how long this Native American Shaman had been working, but there he was, burning sage or some type of herb.

"Excuse me, Wise One, why are you burning all of these herbs?"

"It is my job to burn herbs, to do the cleansing prayers to heal the land. So many dead men. So sad. So hard on the land. All that blood and hatred that the earth takes in. It is bad, so bad."

"Is the energy, the stench of the Civil War what you are trying to cleanse?"

"Yes, have to clean the land. I am caretaker of the land. I must do what I can to clean it. I am here to do my job."

"Have you been here a very long time? Were you here when the war was going on?"

"I do not know. The war goes on and on and I smudge the sage, say the chants, and pray to Okee to heal the land, for the killing to stop."

I gathered that 'Okee' was the name he used to refer to a higher power or his term for God. Since he didn't seem to know how long he had been there, I wasn't sure whether he came after the last group of soldiers was moved on or whether he had been there all along. Perhaps that question is of no consequence. The important issue was my understanding that he had quite a specific mission to complete.

"Day after day, white men kill each other. They are the same just in different clothes, one in blue, one in grey and they kill each other. So much blood, so much death . . ." His voice trailed away as he looked upon a scene that I could not see. The poignancy of his words and the heaviness of his shoulders told me that he was an extremely sensitive soul who had grown profoundly weary of watching man's inhumanity to man.

"I clean the land. The blood goes into ground when men die, when animals die. Great sadness is in blood. Blood in earth is bad for nature and makes a bad place. Violence hurts the land."

I understood exactly what he meant. Darkness from any conflict, be it domestic violence on a small scale to national war on a large scale, brings with it a lingering dark resonance that perpetuates various acts of violence, depression, and death.

We worked together for quite a while to clean that area of land. I think that without a little help, he would have had to burn a veritable mountain of sage to cleanse such a large area as this battlefield. The toxic energies of the butchery of hand-to-hand combat, the death of so many and the sheer force of so much hatred had contaminated the land.

I offered him the use of the ancient resins of Dragon's Blood, Frankincense, Myrrh and Benzoin – all of which work in any dimension. They work much faster and are far more effective than what he was used to using. He seemed grateful for the assistance. It was obvious to me that the Native American sense of responsibility to the land did not end at death.

Once I had assisted him in his mission, I was able to provide him with an angel escort. It was heartwarming to see him finally be welcomed home by other members of his tribe and family. His dedication to the land was remarkable. No one else seems to think of how critical it is to clear the energies of death, violence and tragedy that are the signatures of war. When I shared this information with Shelly, she seemed pleased and acknowledged that the smell of sage was gone now.

Epilogue

Even though Shelly lived in a condo, the stack of time that was having the greatest influence on that entire property was the Civil War. I could not get an exact date, but it would obviously have been between 1860-1865. The Civil War was such a profoundly turbulent time that the energy of the violence, sadness and devastation will linger in the Southern United States for possibly another two hundred and fifty years. The more land that can be cleaned and cleared of this past wartime violence, the calmer and more peaceful will be the people who reside there.

It is important to realize that no specific Civil War battle took place near this woman's condo, although one of the most famous Naval engagements took place at sea near there, the battle between the USS Monitor and the CSS* Virginia (formerly the USS Merrimac). This lack of a nearby battleground caused me to ponder why there would be ghosts from the Civil War there. In fact, I find myself removing many ghosts from Virginia Beach and other parts of Virginia. Perhaps it is because 2200 of the 4000 Civil War battles took place in Virginia. The energy, the sadness, the grief of the Civil War quite literally surrounds this entire area.

Helen Stanton was, and still is, one of the most

courageous women and memorable ghosts I have ever had the privilege of encountering. Her dedication, courage and caring could not be stopped by her physical death. It was heartbreaking to see her wearing the blood-soaked clothes she died in, her own blood and that of the soldiers she so tirelessly cared for night and day. I was amazed to learn that she knew she was dead. She understood that the men she was helping were also dead. And what's even more amazing was that she saw the Light of Transition waiting for her. She could so easily have simply stepped into that light, but she somehow knew that she didn't have the horsepower to bring those men with her, and she was not going to leave without them. Her insight was utterly astonishing. Those men could not transition directly into the light because they simply did not realize that they were dead. For them, the battle still raged. If you don't know you're dead, you don't know you can cross over into the Heaven World.

Hearing her story, her hope for a happier United States and better times was amazing. She was already anticipating a brighter future for those who might live after this heart-breaking time.

The current homeowner's willingness to open the door to assisting, well over two hundred Civil War dead, in addition to the Native American Shaman by asking that her house be cleared of ghosts, was the pure essence of light work. Transitioning this many dead to the Heaven World and clearing the earth of this powerfully contaminated energy is a great spiritual relief that will help the land in the current time enjoy renewed energy. The healing needed for the

Ghost Stories from the Ghosts' Point of View

Civil War to truly be over, took another step forward.

And one final footnote: Shelly told me that she felt desperate to find help whatever or whoever was in her house. One day she walked into a store (a health food and metaphysical store at the beach) and asked where she could find someone to remove ghosts and the clerk pointed to the bulletin board with business cards on it. She walked up to the board, found my sister's Feng Shui business card, and called her that day. The rest is simply remarkable history and service. I believe that Helen directed Shelly to pick up the card. Perhaps Helen saw something through the card. That would explain why she told me that she had 'been waiting for me' when I got to the house. Sometimes, this job can be a bit unnerving.

*CSS stands for Confederate States Ship

On the Wagon Train

Sometimes, when you can see and/or feel the dead, they come to you wherever you are and they beg you to help them. Whether or not you can see or hear them isn't as important to them as whether or not you can actually help them. And so, this hauntingly disturbing situation unfolded.

I was on vacation with my family. We were in Arizona one very cold and snowy December evening, heading into Flagstaff to spend the night. But the road was so thick with snow that we decided to stop immediately at a hotel at the next exit. After a wonderful supper, we were all walking back through the softly falling snow, breathing in the Christmassy air, when I felt as if someone hit me in the chest with a brick. I could not breathe. The intensity of what I was feeling created a most alarming breathing problem.

How could I go from a magical moment in the Flagstaff snow to feeling like I was suffocating? I have unfortunately learned through many a tough time that this must mean that something terrible happened here. The constriction of my airway was becoming frightening. My family became alarmed as I grabbed my throat and rushed back to the hotel to figure out what was surrounding me. I felt a moment of heavy, cold, fear sweep me. My happy moment was gone: I already dreaded what I would find.

Anna Mae

Once I returned to our hotel, I sat down and began to remote view the area outside the hotel (I did not need permission since I was paying to stay in the hotel, and I was only looking at the parking lot outside.)

I immediately saw two little girls. They were adorable children with what must have once been long blond hair. They both had blue eyes. One child was about age five and the other was seven. The five-year old seemed to be the one doing all the talking. The seven-year-old was in complete and utter shock. She appeared totally mute. There was a wild, horrified look in her eyes. Each child was wearing what looked like matching, handmade, pink, and blue gingham dresses, but it was hard to tell, because they were so shredded and thoroughly saturated in blood.

The younger child told me her name was Anna Mae, and she desperately wanted to tell me their story. She just had to tell someone what happened to her family.

"Hurry, the Injuns are gonna' come again! You gots to help us! I keeps asking everyone for help, but they don't help us. Can you see us? Can you help us?"

"Yes, I can see you. What happened here? Where

On the Wagon Train

are your parents?"

"See our parents standin' over there? They keeps staring at their bodies as if they want to try to get back into 'em, but they ain't gonna get back in them bodies. I keep calling to 'em to help us, but they must be frozen where they're standin'. Maybe it was 'cause the Injuns came so quick like.

"As we was travelin' on the wagon train, I asked Papa if there was Injuns nearby 'cause I had a bad feelin'. But papa didn't think there were any Injuns here. But then they come from everywhere, screaming out of the woods! There were arrows flying in all directions! I seed one hit my sister, Belle and she fell. I reckoned she were a-powerful scared when she saw em, like me. I'm guessin' I don't know if she died right then, but truth is, I don't rightly know when she died."

"When did this happen, Anna Mae, day, or night?"

"I reckon it musta' been evenin' 'cause we was just about to set up camp for the night. It was when we stopped that I heared the whoops a-comin'. I 'member I started screaming for papa. Mama tried to hold me and Belle close, but them Injuns, them Injuns was everywhere we looked. There was so many of 'em!

"I'm tryin' to tell folks not to be here but they keeps on a-comin'. Don't they know about them Injuns? How's I gonna' warn people?

"Can you help us? I don't even know what's happened to everyone. I keeps seein' this one Injun coming at me and then it - it starts all over again. I don't understand. This is all so confusin' for me. Can you help me? Light Lady, can you do anythin' to help us?"

I take a very deep breath because I can breathe now.

I could also see a group of Native American Indians in the background with bloody tomahawks in their hands. Near them were wrecked wagons and a group of dead settlers. However, it was these two little girls who seemed to represent the terrible events that had happened to these rugged settlers, these once hopeful families.

These little girls must have been gorgeous, but when they each appeared to me, I saw them at the last electrifying moment, at the ultimate fatal instant of their terrifying deaths. Each enraged Indian attacker had begun to take the scalp off of their heads before either child took their last breaths. Both beautiful little girls had been scalped and stabbed repeatedly, to death. I could also see arrows in their chests. It was a horribly gruesome way to die.

"Anna Mae, yes, I can help you."

There are those times when I fervently wish that I could sweep up the soul in front of me in an enormous loving hug and help them to know that he or she is no longer alone, that their ordeal is finally over. I desperately wanted to hug Belle and Anna Mae. My heart ached for the fear and panic these children had faced. But I am never allowed to do that because neither of us is in physical bodies. All I could do was immediately call in an enormous team of Angels of Transition to begin to assist all of these people who seemed absolutely frozen in time and space. These Indians massacred an entire wagon train of settlers one cold, dusky evening. It appeared to me that the settlers had time to get at least several

On the Wagon Train

shots off because there were dead Indians standing around in this terrified mix of hostile (to each other) souls.

"Do you see all of these bright people coming in, Anna Mae, and helping your family and the other settlers? Can you see that your sister Belle is able to feel that warm wrap around her shoulders? Do you see that there is now someone for each person on your wagon train? Can you feel the light around your shoulders?"

"Yes," she cries softly, "Yes I can see 'em. Yes, I'm feelin' better. I see all kinds of light and folks helpin' us. I'm finally feelin' warm and I'm not so scared no more. Is it time to go? But if I go, who'll warn other wagon trains about them Injuns?"

"I can take care of that. Things are different now. You and all these people are safe from harm. You don't need to worry about them anymore. They'll be just fine, Anna Mae, you've done a wonderful job of trying to help."

"But how come they're givin' help to those Injuns? They don't be deserving of them, causin' they killed us!"

"I have to help everyone I find including the Indians. I don't get to judge anyone. Removing the Indians will also help to make this area safer. You want me to help other wagon trains that would come through here, don't you? Well, to be able to do that I have to help these Indians cross over as well. Do you understand?"

"Well, as long as them Injuns don't hurt good folks no more, then I reckon it's okay."

This precious child turns her face toward the now

almost blinding light and moves toward it, gripping her parents and her sister's hands. But she stops and turns around, waving at me, ever the charming child.

"Goodbye, Light Lady! Thank you! Thank you!"

I turned to help the Indians cross over with their angel escorts and finally, one of them speaks to me, albeit grudgingly.

"Why do they come? Why does the white man think this is his land? Why does he take what is not his? They destroy our food; they take our land, and they massacre the buffalo! Why? Why do they think they can do this? We cannot understand. There can be no peace with thieves."

"Thieves. I understand that this would be how you would have perceived the white man. I feel your sense of outrage. Perhaps the white man thought that there was so much land that there would have been plenty for all. Perhaps there would have been, but the wanton destruction of land, buffalo, rivers, and streams would have appeared as a sacrilege to you."

"No one invited them. They did not ask permission. We did not want their seed, their children to reproduce on our land. No one grieved our children when the white man killed our families. There is no fairness with the white man."

He bowed his head and accepted the assistance offered by the angels as he crossed over. I felt badly that I had no other words of solace.

Once they were all gone, the drama of this scene was finally over.

Epilogue

Anna Mae's demand to know why I brought in

On the Wagon Train

angels for all of the Indians is an important point. While I offered her only the briefest of explanations, there is a far more critical issue here.

The larger explanation is because the Indians were also in pain, emotional pain, rage, and betrayal at the constant theft of their land. They needed help as badly as the settlers did.

My job is not to judge the participants in any drama. My job is to help all participants and to allow the Heaven World to sort out the karma of all of the players in this tragic mortal scene. When you do spiritual work, you don't get to judge, you are required to do your job without prejudice and allow the karmic wheel to turn as it is supposed to – without any interference from the mortal realm. We who assist in this manner are only permitted to do what we are allowed to do by spiritual law, and nothing else. We do not determine whether or not someone is worthy of God's love, or whether they can be allowed to cross into the Heaven World or where someone goes once they leave the 4th dimensional plane. Our job is only to provide assistance, love, and compassion to all.

And with that, the entire event, that drama that happened outside of Flagstaff at least 150 years ago, was finally over. I cannot help but imagine how many people this special child, Anna Mae, approached for help, people who genuinely could not see or hear her. I will always feel fortunate that I was able to help her that night. Here again, this child literally took my breath away with her desire to save people from a similar fate.

On the Wagon Train

The Tennessee Property

I received a call from a long time client and friend. She lives on a gorgeous, wooded piece of property in Tennessee. She hadn't lived there long because she and her husband just recently built a house on this land. However, she spent quite a bit of time by herself at home and began to feel that she was not entirely alone on the premises. She told me she didn't feel anything particularly menacing, just a subtle presence.

Many times, a subtle presence can seem like you see something out of the corner of your eye, you feel a sense of someone there, but you can't be quite sure. The most telling aspect is the feeling that you are never fully alone in your home – but you can't explain this to anyone.

She asked me if I would take a look at all of their eighteen acres and see what I could find. She knew not to tell me anything more. I wanted to have a completely open mind about what I would or would not see. You never know how many stacks of time or souls you will find in any location.

After my initial scan, I was delighted to observe that no wars were ever fought on this spot of land. The Revolutionary War, the War of 1812, The Civil War, and the Spanish American War were all, blessedly, fought elsewhere. Also, there were never slaves on this property. This seemed to be a unique piece of land free of armed conflict.

However, that did not mean these gorgeous, green, wooded rolling hills weren't haunted.

The Last Guardian

He was sitting cross-legged in front of his lodge house, smoking a pipe. The old Shaman was so peaceful sitting there gazing out across the countryside at all the trees. This land had no wires or houses, for the white man hadn't yet begun to settle in these particular mountain areas.

I looked around, hoping to see other tribe members, but he was absolutely alone, nor were there other dwellings. What was one Indian doing with a lone lodge house in the countryside? Where were his tribesmen?

I got his attention and he turned towards me as if seeing someone from a different realm were the most natural thing in the world. The face that greeted me had a very ruddy complexion, deeply lined and full of wisdom and kindness. His flowing white hair and animal skin clothing made him appear that he had just walked out of a unique stack of time or at least an old movie.

"Excuse me, Wise one, are you all alone here?"
"Yes."

The Tennessee Property

"Why are you here by yourself?"

"White man took Cherokee land, and we had no land. All tribe left with Army to a place called 'Okla homa'."

He pronounced Oklahoma in two words, as if the word and the location of Oklahoma were such an alien place to him. Then he bowed his head in abject sadness. I found it almost poignant that he knew his tribe had left him, that he was quite alone.

"How did this happen? Why did this happen?

"Army told tribe chief that President Andrew Jackson, a great white leader, said all Cherokee had to leave tribal land. Said land now belongs to white man. Cherokee have always lived in these lands. We are guardians of the land. We do not understand why we have to leave. All tribe left."

"What was your job in the tribe and why didn't you leave with them?"

"I am Shaman for Cherokee nation." He is very proud of this title, and he explains it to me as if he is currently the Shaman for the entire Cherokee nation.

"Tell me why you stayed here when the others left?"

"The night before tribe leave on trail of disgrace and humiliation I was dying. Tribal elders took me into forest to die peaceful death. They left me with lodge house, so I stay guardian of land of our fathers after life left my body."

"What does it mean to be a guardian of the land?"

"To protect land, to guard it. Cherokee nation always guardians of land. Land good to our people. There was no one before us. Great Spirit put us here to guard land. Land part of our soul. To leave land, sad for tribe. I not leave land. I die and now I guard land."

"What are you protecting the land from?"

"Protect land from those who would hurt land."

What he simply did not realize was that the worst that could happen to the land, had happened. It was the total removal and relocation of the Cherokee Nation in 1838-1839 by the US Army to Oklahoma. That travesty of one group of people on another went down in history as the Trail of Tears.

"Wise One, do you see this glorious one that I have brought with me? He is here to take you home. Your guardian job is finally over. Do you see that light over there?"

"Yes." He stood up with great dignity and faced the angel proudly. The angel gently placed the healing energy around his ancient shoulders and then slowly guided him toward the light.

"I see tribe! Miss them. Lonely here on land. Will land be safe now? Will you watch land for me since it is time to leave?"

"Yes, of course the land will be just fine now because of your guardianship. There is no longer a need for anyone to watch this land. You have done a wonderful job, Wise One, thank you." The angel nodded to me and then he and the dedicated Shaman were gone. Once they left, I could no longer see the lodge house and that entire scene faded.

This Shaman could not see any current day white men. He was frozen in the moments after his tribe left, ever vigilant in his stack of time. Perhaps the final irony is that the land that this Shaman guarded did not see any battles of any American wars. No slavery

The Tennessee Property

took place here. The noble trees of his beloved forest were still standing tall and safe. Perhaps his guardianship was far more effective than he would ever know.

"Can You Tell Me Why?"

The next evening, I went back to scan this property and this time there were no tribal people, but I did find a little girl. I had not seen her previously. She saw me and immediately began a conversation.

"Can you tell me why my Daddy beat me so hard?"

Her long chestnut pigtails framed her thin, bloodied, black and blue face. She must have been so pretty. She seemed to be about eight-years old. Her slight frame wore extremely tired hand-me-down clothes. Her long-sleeved dress hung loosely on her body as she looked at me with a tear-stained face. Her left leg and right arm were eerily hanging at odd angles.

"No, I'm afraid I can't. I need you to tell me more about what happened to you. Can you tell me your name and how you came to be in this house?"

She had seemed so abused when I finally discovered her in my client's kitchen. I needed her to share her obviously violent journey, but I wanted to know who she was and roughly how long ago she had died.

"My name's Jane and I was livin' down yonder in them trailers. I – I see'd this lady, I been watchin' her, and she seems like such a nice lady that I, I come over here cause she seemed so kind. It ain't dark at her house. I jus' wanted to be with a kind person. My family weren't kind. They's mean, real mean to me, mean to everybody."

This poor child was so wounded, on every level: physical, emotional, and even spiritual. All the adults in her life that mattered, had obviously abandoned her. Now she was only looking for kindness.

"Jane, honey, do you know what an angel is? Have you ever seen a picture of one in a book?"

"Yes, I have. They look so pretty."

"Well, I'm sending you a child angel, someone to take your hand so you won't be alone. You don't have to be afraid of being hurt anymore."

"But I'm seeing another little girl with wings. Is she an angel? I thought they were always tall."

"This time, the angel is just your age, and she is bringing you this pretty shawl to wrap around your shoulders. Does that feel nice?"

"Yes, I can feel it. I've been real cold and I'm awful tired. Why don't no one love me? Will the angel hurt me? I don't think I can hold her hand. I must be real bad cause my Daddy beat me so hard and Momma, she jus', she jus'. . ." Jane turns away and her sentence trails off. It's as if she is constantly weeping. She had such a sad heart. This poor child had lost all trust that there could be anyone kind except my client. The child angel gently slips her hand into Jane's and offers a bright smile to warm her heart.

"This angel is going to help you to feel much better, Jane. No harm will come to you, I promise. Tell me about your Momma. What happened in your house that your Daddy beat you and what did your Momma think about this? What did she do?"

"Daddy beat me ne'er every night. He'd come

The Tennessee Property

home drunk and beat me, or Momma. If he was beatin' Momma, I'd try to stop him but if he was a beatin' me, well Momma, I reckon she would just run off and hide. She didn't never try to stop him. He said we was bad and that he had to punish us 'cause God said we was bad. Am I a bad girl? I don't know what I did but when he was powerful drunk, he beat me real hard. He always come in at night and yank me out of bed and scream at me. Sometimes I jus' got slapped but this last time, he punched me with his fists all over my body. I remember that my arm and leg hurt so bad. I ain't never felt pain like that. Finally, everything went black and then I remember wakin' up in this dark place. I don't know where I am, do you? Alls I know is that I can see this kind lady in her kitchen cookin'. She seems so sweet."

"You are in a place, Jane, where sometimes people go temporarily when they die, and I need you to understand that your Daddy did kill you that last time he beat you. This is why I brought in this sweet little angel to help you with the pain you must still be feeling in your body. Are you beginning to feel better now?"

"Yes, it hurt so bad. Momma cried when he kept punchin' me but she jus' stood there cryin'. Guess she figured she couldn't stop him."

I was struck by the flatness of her whisper-like voice, the lack of virtually any emotion, as if she were still in shock, unable to fully grasp that she had died, that in the time of her greatest need, her mother abandoned her in the worst way. Part of me wanted to throw my arms around her and tell her that she would be all better. Sometimes I have to remind myself to stay detached. If I become emotionally drawn into the ghost's story, I am unable to help them. But that doesn't mean that I didn't want to bring her home, take her in, feed her, clothe her, love her, and show her what kindness is like.

But I couldn't do that. The only thing I could do was offer her the compassionate love of an angel and assistance in crossing into the light.

"I suspect that your Momma was pretty afraid of your Daddy. Maybe that's why she didn't defend you. For now, the pain, the fear and the dread are over. I'm glad you found this nice lady. Her name is Cari and she asked me to see if anyone in her house needed help. You were right to trust that she was a kind person because she truly is."

Jane was looking better and better as the healing coat began to remove the pain of all of those brutal blows. When she looked at her companion angel she was beginning to smile. I asked her if she was ready to go with this angel to a beautiful place.

"Yes, I think so if it's okay. Are there nice people there, at this place I'm goin' to?"

"Yes, honey, there are very nice people there. And now the angel is going to escort you to your real home in the Heaven World. Goodbye, sweet Jane."

I nodded to the angel and hand-in-hand the child and the angel slipped effortlessly into the welcoming light. I took a very deep breath and sent her prayers of hope and love.

I wondered how much more there could be on these 18 acres.

"I Should Have Paid More Attention."

The Tennessee Property

I checked back the next night and again scanned the property. No more Indians, no small children and yet I could still feel that there was someone still here.

"Can you see me?"

"Yes, sir, I can see you. How in the world did you come to be in Cari's house?"

"I was crossing the street in downtown Norfolk (Virginia) while I was talking on my cell phone and I must not have been paying attention and some woman, who I gathered as I stood next to the police trying to explain what happened to me, said that she was on a cell phone too. Can you believe it? She's not paying attention on her phone and I'm not paying attention on my phone! I was in a hurry to a meeting and the next thing I know I'm flying through the air into absolute blackness. It was so quick! Oh, excuse me, let me introduce myself, I'm Jonathan Jones, CPA."

"Well Mr. Jones, CPA, how did you end up at this house in the mountains of Tennessee?"

"I don't know exactly. I just know that I had no idea what to do once I finally figured out that I was dead. I wandered and felt more and more confused in this land of gray. I kept seeing these shadowy figures and then in the distance, I saw something that was brighter than the gray and I followed it. I ended up with this lady here. I'm not sure what I'm doing here, just waiting, I guess. I have no idea what's happening. Are you here to help me?"

Talk about confused! This poor man needed to understand more about where he was and what needed to happen to him. His three-piece suit was wrinkled, damp from the blood that seeped from his injuries. He looked bruised and battered. I gathered from talking to him that he literally never knew what hit him. One minute he is on his way to a meeting and the next he is sailing through blackness utterly confused.

"Sir, you are correct that you did die on that street, and you followed this woman's light. She must have been visiting friends or something when you saw her. Anyway, she is a kind person and has brought me here to assist you. I've brought in someone to help you. Do you see him?"

"Yeah, I do. Not too sure I believe in angels. How's this work? I'm not too religious. Never much went to church. Is there really a God?"

'Yes, Mr. Jones, there very definitely is a God and whether or not you went to church is of no importance right now. Angels don't concern themselves with that. Their job is to act as your escort to the Heaven World. Can you feel the warmth that's surrounding you?"

"Yes, and oddly, I am feeling much warmer. I've been so cold for so long that I guess I got used to it. Do I just go with this big guy? Forgive me, but frankly, he's a bit intimidating. Is that how it works? And then what happens? Where does he take me? I guess I'm still feeling a bit uncertain about this process."

"This angel escort is going to help you cross over into the light of the Heaven World. Then he will take you to a place that will provide some initial healing based on your method of death. After that, what happens is based on all kinds of factors, but I can assure you that you will encounter a great deal of kindness. Please understand that you are safe in this process." I nod to the angel and then Mr. Jones is gone.

Cari's Kindness

I scanned this property one more night and finally it was completely free of ghosts, or at least the ghosts that were allowed to be presented to me at the time. Then I called my client.

"Hi Cari, how are things feeling now?"

"Oh, so much better. They didn't feel bad, or evil, but I kept feeling there was someone here and now that feeling is utterly gone. I'm alone on the property with my husband and pets."

"Well, you had three fascinating if somewhat tragic characters." I then proceeded to tell her about each one.

"I'm curious, did the Shaman see me? Did all those other people see me?"

"The Shaman couldn't see you. He was completely stuck in his stack of time and was already on the property many dozens of decades before you arrived. I suspect you didn't really feel him. Moving him on was simply a spiritual bonus. However, Jane and Mr. Jones specifically sought you out, so your own lovely light attracted them. You would have definitely felt their presence. Neither of them was bad nor evil. Jane's death was pretty terrible, but Mr. Jones died in a cell phone/traffic accident. Although this was also very sad, he was not abused prior to his death. His death was not a physical torture in and of itself. I got the impression that Jane lived nearby. Any thought as to where she came from?"

"There is a group of depressed houses/trailers not far from me. Maybe she came from there. That's the closest group of people to me. Mr. Jones, gee I could have picked him up before I left Norfolk several years ago. Anyway, it doesn't matter. So glad you were able to help them all."

"Yes, it's always gratifying to help any soul and it's wonderful to know that they could see the light of your goodness."

Epilogue

It is not unusual to see several different ghosts on a piece of property separated by stacks of time. None of these ghosts could see each other. They were each in their own world, their own time and in their own, individual emotional place yet they were all in the 4th dimension.

The situation on Cari's property is an excellent example of the presence of predecessor energy from the Cherokee Indians. However, the other two ghosts were simply attracted to Cari's spiritual light. They had never lived on this land.

Cari's goodness helped them all even though she didn't know it when it was happening. Her desire to make sure that the land was cleared and that anyone on the land received help was truly a beautiful act of kindness.

Her Sorrowful Heart

The Eastern Shore of Virginia is a quiet, peaceful and restful place. It has a National Park and wildlife refuge with a beautiful heavily wooded, winding trail that takes you past enchanting butterfly meadows to the fragrant marshland of the inland waterway. On this path to the Atlantic, you walk through lush forests filled with woodpeckers, robins, box turtles, and deer. It is such an abundant location. The oak, elm, sycamore, and pine trees meet the salt marsh and give ground to a waving sea of golden grasses, about chest high. These lush grasses that make up this salt marsh provide a seafood bounty for snowy egrets, blue herons, and sea gulls. This area isn't exactly a beach but more of a low country type of marsh. It's somewhat underwater when the tide comes in but when the tide's out, there are all kinds of mud-loving creatures that give life to this thriving stretch of the Chesapeake Bay. It's gorgeous as it stretches out before you to the sapphire sea. The warm summer air is soft, comforting and inviting.

But it wasn't always this way. In the winter of the very early 1700s, it was bitter cold and uninviting. The headstones in the pitiful, small cemetery several yards from the water's edge bear mute testimony to the many souls who never made it through the brutal winters on this edge of the Atlantic Ocean as the fledgling settlements of the New World were just getting started.

Elizabeth Ann Jackson

In each of the many times I have walked these trails I have removed ghosts. However, this time, the ghost who approached me told me that she needed help.

"I've seen you here before. I watched you send on the other settlers, but I hid away from this little graveyard. I – I wasn't ready to go. I wasn't worthy to go into that light you send folks to when you find them."

I am quite surprised to see her. She is a frail woman in colonial dress. Her long, shabby beige skirt and prim blouse show tremendous wear, almost as if this were the only piece of clothing she had ever owned. Her dark tattered, wool shawl is ineffective against the cold she seems to be feeling. I can see her peering at me from behind one of the worn headstones before she stands up and comes toward me.

I get the distinct feeling that she wants me to hear her story, to understand why she has waited all this time. Sometimes patience will enable you to know the heart of a ghost if you are willing to listen.

Her Sorrowful Heart

"Can you tell me your name?"

"I am Elizabeth Ann Jackson and I need you to understand that I want your help, but I don't know how to ask for it. I am not worthy of God's love. I am not worthy of that light. Those other women who died went on to see Jesus, but I don't think even Jesus would have a place for me."

The intense power of her sorrowful heart was tremendous. I couldn't imagine what would have caused her such guilt. She was obviously an extremely religious woman from her references to Jesus. I urged her to continue.

"I'm not sure how I did it, but I think I killed my sweet baby girl."

She looked away from me in intense shame. I wanted so much to wrap her in unconditional love. My sense was that she did not kill her child. My feeling was that something else happened and she was blaming herself.

"Elizabeth, please, it's alright now, can you tell me what happened? There's no judgment here, there's only the hope that you can find a way to heal. Please tell me."

"It's cold here, so cold. I, we, none of us were prepared for the winters here. There was so little to eat, we haven't been here too long, and we don't know what is safe in the forest to eat and the forest is so thick. Some other colonists ate something from the woods and died, their faces full of pain. Some of the other women got so cold that they came down with a powerful fever. We didn't know what plants we could use to heal us, to bring the fire out of our bellies.

"Some of our women died and so did their babies.

We buried them here in this cemetery. I look out for the babies – now that I'm dead too.

"We didn't know what we could eat. We didn't realize how much food we would need to put aside for the winter months. Winter goes on so long here, not like England. It's so cold every single day and the rain hurts when it comes down, like it's ice. It stabs your face.

"I got pregnant not long after we got here when there was food, when we thought we would be able to live here. The men, they killed deer and rabbit, but we couldn't keep the food, no way to preserve it and in the winter, there wasn't enough game. We were hungry all the time. It gnaws on your belly so badly."

She looks away for a minute as if she is recalling her pain.

"When the leaves fell off the trees, it got cold. I think I was about three or four months into carrying my baby. As each month came, I got more and more hungry and there was less and less to eat. More and more women died. If they had babies, their babies died too. See, here are Elijah, Josephus, Benjamin, and Catherine Carter. All these babies are dead and I'm taking care of them. Some of them made it to two years old.

"My baby came way too early, and she was born dead. I knew I had killed her somehow. Babies are not supposed to die when you birth them. My little girl Bethany, she was named after me, is buried here too. I – I think I'm a bad person because I must've killed her."

I watched as her slight shoulders began to heave with the tremendous grief-filled sobs that come with the loss of a child. That pain is so merciless that there are no words to describe it. My heart went out to her. Here she is practically starving and freezing to death herself and she ends up blaming herself for the death of her own baby.

"Elizabeth, please tell me what caused your death. Do you know?"

"My husband, John, said I had to 'get over' the loss of our baby. I don't know how to do that. Something alive inside of me is dead and it must be my fault. I grieved so much and the only small comfort I had was to go and lie on my baby's grave in the soft snow. Each time my husband would come and find me and bring me back home, but one night I refused to leave, and I guess he just gave up. He let me stay, and as the snow covered my body, I froze to death on her grave. John buried me next to baby Bethany.

"Now I watch over the babies because I can see them all. I read the Bible all my life and now that I'm dead, I don't recall the Bible ever talking about what happens to dead babies. I could see them and there were no angels with them or light. I just knew I had to stay with them to look out for them in this terrible darkness."

"Why are you asking me for help now, Elizabeth?"

"Because I'm so terribly cold, tired and I'm too weary to take care of these babies any longer and I'm asking you for help."

I can already see the angels gathered around each baby. Each little soul is gently, lovingly wrapped in the softest 'receiving' blanket. The blankets look like the finest, gossamer fabric; they are filled with the energy of the warmth of divine light, and they spiritually revive each dear little child. This blessed energy brightens their souls, and they start to send Elizabeth their love for caring for them for so long.

"I can't believe that the light has finally come for us. Could this angel actually be for me? Is this blanket really for me? Did you ask God to forgive me? Can God forgive me?"

"Yes, Elizabeth, all this is for you. It is the very nature of God to forgive, and He has already forgiven you. God understands the terrible conditions you were living in during these early days of those settlements. Please remember that you have always been loved, and the divine light and love of Jesus is waiting for you and all of these babies. Do you see the other colonists who are ready to greet you on the other side?"

She looked into the warm, welcoming light and the relentless cold and fatigue that had so endlessly dogged her seemed to leave her exhausted ghostly frame. She looked back at me briefly and then resolutely walked into the light with the bright angel by her side. The families of all the babies met the angels who were carrying their small children. It was truly a glorious reunion.

Epilogue

The issue of why the light did not come for the babies is important to understand. Often when a child dies from such severe privation, the child is not aware of what to do at death. This is truly a terrible situation. Even people today do not realize that they can ask for angels to take their children to the Heaven World in any situation in which a child dies.

Her Sorrowful Heart

Elizabeth's guilt held her here and by taking care of those ghost children, she was in her own way atoning for the death of her precious little girl. Even though someone watching this situation would not feel that she had done anything to engender such guilt, the soul feels what it feels. When she was ready for the situation to end, help was provided.

It's been over 300 years since Elizabeth Ann Jackson died. The winters on the Eastern Shore of Virginia are no longer as severe as they were then. Sleet, the frozen rain she spoke of, now only comes occasionally and snow is a rarity in these times. I often marvel that any of the original colonists made it through the brutal winters of the New World.

In essence, Elizabeth died of starvation and severe grief. Her sorrowful heart could no longer bear the continual loss of child after child in their tiny intimate community. One woman's loss was every woman's loss. She finally lost all hope when her own child was stillborn. Those precious children were the promise of tomorrow and when all hope dies, something dies inside you.

Perhaps we would be wise to remember the staggering contribution as well as the sacrifice of colonists like John and Elizabeth Jackson. It is my fervent prayer that the angels will bless and keep all of these settlers through time and eternity.

Her Sorrowful Heart

The Dallas Cowboys

They thought they grew up.
They thought they grew past the need for their mother.
They thought they didn't need the things that reminded them of their happy times in childhood.
They didn't realize that they ended up following the admonishments of their mother. Mostly, they weren't conscious of how this works; they just longed for that feeling they had, when they felt safe at home.

Often at death, it is the comfort of a person's mother that a soul seeks. When she can't be found, there is a stubborn sadness, a longing for that feeling of coming home. So, the soul seeks a place that can fill that deep emotional void.

"We Think Our House is Haunted."
I received a referral call from a couple that I had never met. They owned a gorgeous piece of property in Dallas, Texas where they built a brand-new home. I'm sure you can well imagine their astonishment at discovering that their home was haunted. When they called me, they were hesitant at first to tell me this fact. Most people are embarrassed to admit what they

are feeling when it comes to addressing the supernatural.

"We got your name from a friend of ours who says that you removed a ghost from her house in New York. We, my husband Tom, and I, we, well, we think our house is haunted, Tina, and we need you to do whatever it is y'all do in these kinds a cases."

Sandy was straightforward yet almost hesitant in her request when we finally spoke. I loved her light Texas drawl.

"Alright Sandy, no problem. What's your address?"

"Is that it? Don't you want to know what's been happening here? I mean do ya just believe us? Don't we have to prove to ya what we've been feelin'?"

"No, not really. If you've gotten up the courage to call me in the first place, you're usually pretty sure about it. I don't ever question someone who asks me to clear a haunted house. I find what I find. Also, if you tell me too much information up front, you'll never know if what I find is because it is a reflection of what you've said at the outset or if it's because I really located the ghost and facilitated that ghost's transition. I won't just be confirming or denying the presence of a ghost. I'll be removing any souls who I find. Will this work for you and Tom?"

"Yes, okay, that's fine, I guess. Here's our address. Will we notice anything? I mean this is just so strange for us. Our pastor said that we must have imagined it all but let me tell you that..."

"Sandy, please, I just know you're bursting to tell me what has been happening, but again, I beg your patience until I can complete my work."

She lets out a sigh. "All right then. Get back to us

real soon, won't you please?"

"Absolutely."

Momma Said . . .

This gracious Texas home had the energetic look and feel of a new house, with new energy. Therefore, it didn't take long to locate 'the boys,' four of them to be exact, because their energy was so out of place. These were big men, or they must have been big men in mortal life because they were enormous ghosts. They were all well over six feet tall with large frames, all wearing big cowboy hats, guns, and chaps, as if they had just gotten off their horses. And they were all soaking wet. They had on various colors of the same type of plaid shirts. It almost looked like they were two sets of twins they looked so much alike. However, I was soon to discover that they were not twins at all, just four very large brothers.

"Howdy, ma'am."

"Well, hello to you too. Who are you guys, and do you realize that you are all huddled in this little, tiny bathroom?"

"Yes ma'am, we do. We gonna stay outta the way in here and then come out when we reckon it's okay or when we ain't gonna be botherin' nobody in the house."

"Who are you guys?"

"We're the Mackenzie brothers, the four of us. Actually, this is our property. We ain't rightly sure who these folks are but they make a nice place, and we like it here."

"They 'make a nice place'? Can you please explain: what does this mean?"

"Well, the misses in this here house has a kitchen and a cook stove a whole lot like our Momma done have way back when we was kids. We sure do like the way this place feels, kinda like bein' back home with our Momma in Alabama. We come from Alabama, way back before the war."

"Which war, Mr. Mackenzie? Did you die in whatever war that was? I'm just curious what happened to all of you guys."

"No, ma'am. We lived through the war, the Civil War. We done growed up in Alabama and when them Yankees started pouring into the South when the war started, we all joined up. Our Momma was real scared for us to be in the War Between the States so she told us how we was gonna survive. She said we was always to stay together no matter what. Me and the boys, all said goodbye to her and then we joined up with General Lee and we made it all the way through the Civil War and nary a one of us was wounded.

"We went home to Alabama, but Momma died during the war, not sure how, we just come home to find a grave with her name on it. We knowed we couldn't stay in 'bama no more, so we sold what we could and cleared out. We headed to Texas to make a fresh start. Momma said we was to stay together so when we got to this here land, we bought 10,000 acres and put up a house, bought us some cattle and started our ranch. It was the Four Circle Ranch. One circle for each of us."

"Did any of you ever marry?"

"Naw, since all four of us survived the Civil War, we done figured it was 'cause a what our Momma said, that we lived 'cause we all stuck together, and

The Dallas Cowboys

we didn't want no woman comin' between us. And it worked - for a while."

"Did a woman come between any of you?"

"Naw. It weren't that. We never was interested in no women. We was just ranchers, and we done real good with the ranch 'til them rustlers come. We had a bad time, us and all them other ranchers in the area. We had no real law man we could go to, and this territory is so big that there weren't no way any law man could cover that much of anybody's land. We worked so hard for what we got but them rustlers were stealin' us blind."

"What finally happened?"

"Ma'am, it was powerful bad. One night it was rainin' so hard we could hardly see to guide our horses, but we figured this'd be just the night the rustlers would be a comin' to steal our Longhorns. And we was right. That night all four of us went out and we decided to split up and we separated, going in four different directions. I reckon that them rustlers musta' been watchin' because we no sooner split up and started out to the far corners of the ranch than them rustlers picked us off one by one. We all died within a few minutes of each other. It was bad. I'm the oldest and I forgot what Momma said. We split up and iffin' we'd stayed together I reckon they couldn't a killed us that way. We shoulda' done what Momma said. I feel real bad about it, real bad. I guess I let everybody down."

He stood there shaking his head and looking down to where his feet would have been. As the oldest son, he felt the responsibility of looking out for all of his brothers and in this he felt he had failed them and his mother. His despair was profound. His brothers never said a word, as if they were so close that they were of one voice, one mind. They all stood there in the rough garb they were wearing when they died, their clothes still dripping wet.

"I'm so sorry that this happened this way to all of you. Tell me, are you able to see the new homes here? How did you pick this house?"

"This was where our ranch house was, but it got torn down. Looks like somebody built this place on that land. It feels real fine in this house. That kitchen has all the stuff our Momma used to have in her kitchen. You know, the baskets, the pitchers we used for milk, even the colors remind us of our Momma. We miss her so much. She even cooks food our Momma used to cook: grits, cookies, corn on the cob, and chocolate cake. She ain't got no cow, but she gets milk from the chill box. She even has Texas wildflowers in a vase on her rough wood kitchen table. Ma'am, it feels like home here to us. We don't rightly know her name, but this here lady is mighty fine, real nice-like and kind. She's real kind to everybody and I reckon, even to us."

"Well boys, the reason I'm here is to help you find your Momma. Do you see those four big angels over there with blankets? Just now they are going to be putting these dry blankets around your shoulders. When you can feel the warmth from them, please let me know."

I nod to the angels to go ahead and place the blankets around the brothers. Immediately I can see all four men brighten and begin to smile.

"Ma'am we're feelin' better, warmer. We did get

tired of being cold, wet, and alone. We ain't never seen no angel before. What do we do with 'em?"

"Ah! It's what they do with you. Gentlemen, are you ready to leave this half-hearted existence and crossover into the Heaven World? Are you ready to see your Momma again?"

"Ma'am, you ain't got no idea how much we would love to see our Momma again." He said this in such a flat, exhausted tone that I almost wondered how they had hung on this long. I nod to the angels to go ahead and take them across into the light of healing, love, and hope.

"Gentlemen, good luck to you." I then caught a glimpse of the four of them crossing over together, almost as if they were one soul. And then there she was, their mother, arms outstretched somehow embracing all four of her enormous sons at the same time. She looked so small and frail and yet she must have appeared as a giant to them. Their reunion was such a joyous event! I could well imagine her anxiety at sending all four of her beloved sons to serve in the Civil War, never knowing if they would survive or what would happen to them. Now, at last they could be together again.

Once they had all been reunited, there was a glorious feeling of happiness and peace that seemed to envelope this beautiful Texas property.

Epilogue

I checked back and those were the only ghosts I ever found in my client's home. Time to call them and tell them what I found.

"Hi Sandy, I've finished with the scan of your

Ghost Stories from the Ghosts' Point of View

home."

"Oh my gosh, we're so excited! What did you find? Were there ghosts? Where they evil or nice? Where were they?" She put me on her speakerphone and called her husband Tom over to listen.

"No, you and your husband weren't crazy, you had four ghosts, four brothers. They loved your home, especially your very homey and warm kitchen. However, how you decorated that space completely reminded these brothers of their mom's kitchen and it was the only peace they could find. They hung out in your downstairs guest bathroom most of the time, the one in that narrow hallway just past the kitchen. . . and yes, I have definitely moved all of them on."

"I knew it! I always felt someone was watching me in that bathroom, so I never used it. It gave me the creeps, I always felt shivers – you know how people say that their hair stood up on the back of their neck, well that's what happened to me. Oh, and I never wanted to look in the bathroom mirror either. I was afraid that I would see someone standing behind me. No one believed me that there were ghosts in the bathroom. It's so amazing that they told you they all hid in the bathroom. I finally feel vindicated! I never felt them anywhere else in the house either. I mean Tom sort of believed me, didn't you honey. Anyway, were these guys murdered? Were they murderers?"

"Oh no, they weren't murderers. They were just four brothers who survived the Civil War but couldn't survive the ravages of the brutality of cattle rustling. One rainy night, rustlers picked each of them off one by one. The only peace they found was being near your kitchen. They were most glad to be able to leave that bathroom, crossover and be with their mother again. It was quite the reunion."

"So, what we did was actually helpful for them? I mean it's okay to remove a ghost?"

"Oh yes, Sandy, it is. You did all four of them quite a service by facilitating their transition. Really, it was wonderful for them. No ghost is ever at peace. The peace of release can only fully come when a soul crosses over. You did really well by them. In true Texas style, you helped them in a very big way."

The Dallas Cowboys

The Oneida Shaman

I get calls from all over the country to help with ghosts. I never know just what I will find. Personally, I find it an honor to get to help so many souls. Usually, homeowners just want what appears to be a haunting to cease, so they can live on 'their' property in peace. I guess the irony is that what we think we own, what we think is 'ours' may have just as rightly belonged to someone else in another time and that person or ghost still believes that the land is 'theirs.' Sometimes though, those souls who may have lived and died on that parcel of earth have a deep emotional hurt that isn't healed, and it doesn't heal no matter how much time passes.

In this case, this homeowner unwittingly performed a tremendous act of kindness by allowing me to assist those souls that were stuck in a sad stack of time on her property, somewhere in upper state New York.

The Initiating Call

"Hi, my name is Evelyn. A friend gave me your name as someone who can remove ghosts."

"Yes, I have been known to have helped a few

ghosts in my time. How can I help you?"

"I just know my house is haunted. I have had all kinds of mediums come out and they all agree that it's haunted, but they tell me that they can't move them on. I want them gone. Should I tell you what's been going on here? I mean, how much detail would you like to know?"

"None, actually. I don't need any detail, because how will you ever know if what I'm seeing is because of what you told me or because of what is really there? So no, don't tell me anything else."

"Is that it? It feels weird not to tell you what's happening here."

"I understand, but at the same time, it's an ethics issue. Let me see what I find and then later you can tell me what was happening."

"Alright, I'll email you the address. How long will it take? Will I feel anything?"

"It takes as long as it takes, usually a couple of days. It also depends on how many other requests I have. I'll let you know. And whether or not you'll feel or sense anything I have no way of knowing. Some people do, some don't."

"I'm excited to see what you find."

"Great! I'll get back to you."

A Truly Sad Stack of Time

When I remote view a property, I can see it as it looks today and then I look for the initiating event in the influencing stack of time.

I take my time. Sometimes it can take literally hours of focus for the influencing stack of time on a particular piece of property to appear. Usually there is

The Oneida Shaman

an originating event that then echoes out through time and space. That's what I'm looking for and patience is required to find it and find it I do.

It's misty, cold, and dark. I've sifted back through almost four hundred years of time stacks. The land looks so different in this time. It's hard to believe how many trees are here, millions of them, so lush and green. There is very little open space because the dense hardwood trees tower over the lodge type homes that I am beginning to glimpse. Slowly, slowly the scene unfolds, and I begin to identify people, Native American Indians who were here originally. It looks like an entire tribe of them. Scanning the area reveals what must have been somewhat sophisticated buildings on this land. However, all that is left are the ribs of their domed wood and mud dwellings. It's almost as if I can smell the smoke from the campfires, or are these the fires that destroyed their homes? Something tragic happened here. I can also see some ash-charred remnants of what must have been settler's homes as well. It almost looked like some unknown force attacked them all.

As I take in the scene, a man comes toward me. He may be the spokesman for the tribe coming to speak to me. He's not the chief; he must be the Shaman. The Shaman is the spiritual advisor for the entire tribe. He may also be the Medicine Man, helping to heal physical and emotional wounds. The term Shaman is one of great respect. Usually these men are very proud, peaceful, and wise. However, this Shaman was anything but peaceful.

This man seems so angry. He has hundreds of Indian souls behind him. I do not see any settlers.

Ghost Stories from the Ghosts' Point of View

"Who are you? What are you doing here? Who said you could come on our land? What do you want? This is our land. You have no right to be here!" He said fiercely.

"I've come to see what happened here. Can you help me?" I appealed to what I hoped would be the helpful side of his nature. He didn't come across as a mean or evil man, just someone who was very angry. I could only imagine how odd it must be for him to see someone like me appearing to him, literally out of nowhere.

"What happened?! The white man is what happened here! This was our land, and they came and took what they wanted. They did not ask. They just took. We tried to be welcoming, but eventually they just took and took from us."

His words, although angry, sounded more like heartbreak and betrayal. I could feel the power of his sense of injustice. I believed him to be basically a peaceful man, a spiritual soul trapped in a terrible situation.

"I'm new here, can you give me a bit more detail? I can see your tribe by you, and they also look so sad. Please tell me how things came to be so bad for you? Everyone looks so ill, all of you."

"I see people where you come from, from your time. We defend our land from so many white men. We will not leave! This is our land, and we have a right to be here! We keep hoping that the English will leave but they come, more and more of them!"

What is amazing is that he can actually see current time from his vantage point almost four-hundred years ago. I gather that the more non-native

Americans he watches over time, the more his resentment grows. His rage is building a tinderbox of powerful negative energy. He is actually aware of his conscious actions because he knows he is trying to influence the people living on the property in this current time.

He lived somewhere in the late 1600s, but his actions are influencing current time in the 21st century. This is how powerful the energy of a ghost can be: their actions can penetrate through hundreds of years and influence current time. If, as Professor Einstein believed, all time is happening at the same time then the energy of a ghost can and does influence living people in current time.

"Your frustration is growing. Are you the one who has been trying to get this homeowner's attention?"

"Yes, but this is not her land! This is our land – our land! I talk to her, and she does not listen."

"I do know that she has asked several other mediums to come and speak to you, so perhaps she is hearing you. Did you hear these others seeking to communicate with you?"

"Yes, they see me, but they do not hear me. No one hears me! – except you. You meet me on my terms, on my land. The others. . . are worthless. Why are you here?"

As I am speaking to this ghost, this almost 400-year-old ghostly soul, I have this feeling of intense compassion begin to sweep me. He is poignantly courageous in his own way, staunchly fierce in his demeanor and he seems grudgingly grateful that he finally has someone who can hear him. I feel honored to have this astonishing opportunity to speak to him.

Ghost Stories from the Ghosts' Point of View

"I'm here to help you and your fellow tribesmen in any way I can."

"Ha! I do not believe you," he tells me flatly.

"Please, at least tell me your story all the way, from when the English and French first arrived to how you all died."

As he is remembering what happened, I take this opportunity to quietly and discretely bring in teams of angels to begin to transition his people to the Heaven World. I notice how appreciative each person is to be able feel the warm embrace of that healing wrap and then to finally slip into that beautiful light that so brightly welcomes each of them. Most of them are each wearing the clothes in which they died: their original clothes of animal skins. But some are wrapped in clothes that do not look like the Indians made them. I can see that their once strong bodies are covered in terrible sores. Even their children have these hideous sores. It looked like each person was still in tremendous pain. Eventually, all of his tribe slipped into the dimensions of the Heaven World.

As the Shaman begins to talk, he barely seems to notice that finally, we are alone on this lonely, chilled, and sad plane of existence.

"I am Shaman of the Oneida tribe in the land the English call New York. But several hundred seasons past, this was not New York it was the land of the Oneida Indians. My people and our ancestors live here for as long as we count time. When the white man came, we lived with them as brothers sharing our land. We taught them how to survive in the cold, to hunt, to fish great rivers and how to honor our land.

"My people were peaceful. We did not want war.

The Oneida Shaman

We did not fight the English because they needed our knowledge to live on our land. The settlers wanted peace and they came to our camp, and we went to their camp. We all worked in peace. Our children, their children played in peace."

"But more and more settlers came, didn't they?"

"Yes, our bothers by the sea told us that big ships came bringing many new people. We not understand how so many people could continue to come. They built more and more houses. Not all of newcomers welcomed our help. Many of the new people were disrespectful to our people, to our ways and our friendship."

He showed me the houses where the settlers lived. This particular house he shows me, was actually an overlay house on the property I was asked to clear. Literally, the energy of this original settler house was having a most powerful influence on the current property and its residents.

"We worry about the new Englishmen who kept coming but we kept trying to work with them. Then one day, new settlers arrived. These new English were different from the other ones. These families were sick. These settlers brought blankets to trade with us. The blankets had evil in them. Sick settlers used them and then give them to us and then we had the same sickness they did. Our bodies got hot with fever. Sores with blood in them came on our bodies. We had never seen this terrible sickness before."

I deduced that the blankets may have been infected with the disease. Perhaps the sick people used the blankets at sea. At this point, we will never know. When the Indians met the colonists, the

Ghost Stories from the Ghosts' Point of View

disease could have been passed by many methods.

"What did you do?"

"I am Shaman, medicine man, but I did not know this horrible sickness. How could I help my people? I watch. Some white families got better, and some did not. My people died. Nothing I did helped them. No herbs worked. The settlers betrayed me. My people no longer believed in me. I failed them all. Mothers blamed me for the death of their children. Husbands blamed me for the deaths of their wives and families.

"My people died. All suffered and cried, and I did know not how to help them. As they died, I saw them stand by their bodies, angry that silent death took them. There was no honor in a death like this. No good death for a warrior, or for chief. When our tribe's children died, I died inside. Fathers and mothers died inside. The English did not help us to heal. White man only helped us to bury our dead. The settlers died, we died and then there was fire all around.

"The English said that to stop the sickness, we had to burn all our homes. I watched all of our lives go up in flames. The settlers' homes were also destroyed by fire. They burned all they had and all we had."

The enormity of the tragedy seemed overwhelming to him. It was as if the entire identity of the tribe was completely destroyed.

"Who will know us? All that we were – gone, our customs, our ways, the knowledge we would pass on to our children: all gone in the fires.

"The settlers also burned all the bodies of their dead to kill the sickness. I watched as the fire was all around me and I felt I was in the land of great evil. Is sickness that killed my people my fault? Should we

The Oneida Shaman

have helped the French and the English?

"I watched as all of my tribesmen died. Watching my tribe's children look up at me with their faces full of pain broke my heart. I was powerless to help them. There was nothing left for me to do. The sickness killed me last. Can you understand my sorrow? Can you understand my rage? I did not want more English families on our land. I wanted our land back. I want my tribe to be back the way it was. . . the way it was when I knew what to do."

As this Medicine Man is sharing these details, his voice becomes softer and softer, until it is almost a whisper. This Shaman's heart was profoundly broken. He loved his people. He had learned to tolerate and accept his new neighbors and now he felt the ultimate betrayal. He could not contain his rage and sorrow. What he could not have known was that the colonists may have had an immune system, which could withstand Smallpox. The Indians would not have had any immune system defenses. The settler's immune systems were simply different. That said, probably hundreds of those families also died.

When a soul has not only a physical responsibility but also a spiritual responsibility to a group of people, he does not stop feeling that weight of accountability for what happens to each person, especially children, when any of them dies. He will continue to feel that burden long after he dies. And it is that guilty feeling that he has failed his people that will hold him on that 4th dimensional plane indefinitely or until he believes that he can ask for and/or be worthy of help. Telling this man that what happened was not his fault will not change how he feels.

I requested an Archangel for this Shaman. He needed the special assistance and spiritual wisdom offered by an Archangel to work through the grief, guilt, and despair of such a tragic spiritual life. These powerful feelings had dramatically lowered his frequency, thereby making it difficult for him to cross over. When a soul feels this broken, this devastated, death is not a release. It's a continual torture. His story, his dedication to his people and the land truly moved me.

"Do you see this Archangel I have brought for you? Go with him, feel the love of the light, and know that you did not fail your people. You gave them the best leadership you possibly could in extraordinarily difficult circumstances. There is no judgment here, only peace."

I watched as the Shaman left. He looked back at me for a moment, looked up at his divine escort and then he was gone.

Persistent Fire Energy

The house I was there to clear had been one of those that was reduced to cinders during that time to clear it of disease. As I continued to scan the property through the stacks of time, I noticed that in other more recent time stacks whatever house had been on this property had also burned. The energy of fire persists for hundreds of years unless someone works to clear the property of fire energy.

I could also see that there had been a small fire in the house that is currently there, so I cleared this energy as well. Simply assisting the Indians to transition was a huge step in clearing this land. I helped all the souls I could see, all who came for help. I assisted the entire tribe to transition to the Heaven World, to receive healing and compassion. Then I gave healing to the land itself. When the Earth receives healing, it is as if you can hear this wonderful sigh of relief. And so, it was here. I knew that things would be better on this area of the earth.

Epilogue

Several days later I called Evelyn and told her the story of this sad and courageous Shaman.

"So that's the story."

"I had no idea all this was here but oh, you are so right about the fires. There has been a history of fires on this property, so that almost unnerved me when you shared that part of the story. And I never told you about the fire we had in the kitchen. Funny, when the fire started, we were all pretty angry at that moment!"

"In unusual cases, fires can start through the anger of one person. But any fire is greatly facilitated by the predecessor energy of fire and rage. How do things feel now?"

"Oh, things feel so much better. It's so hard to quantify. It's as if the house finally feels at peace, and I feel alone in my own house. I kept feeling like someone was here, like there was a presence, a powerful male presence, menacing, but not menacing. I can't explain it. Do you understand?"

"Yes, I do, on many levels. I also want to thank you for helping these souls to move on. I can't help them unless a property owner asks me for help."

"Thank you. This feels so much better! I felt so frustrated that several different mediums identified that there was a ghost here, but no one could get him to leave."

"You are most welcome. If you would, could you please send these Indians your prayers for a while? I believe it would help them quite a bit."

"I would be happy to do that."

It is often hard to imagine what could be on a specific piece of property and perhaps that is how it is meant to be. We each have an opportunity to make our property so much better in so many ways and help countless souls we have never met. I was delighted to know that Evelyn could feel the difference. Perhaps now this modest section of Earth can be at peace for a very long time.

The Witness Protection Program

Sometimes fear is your greatest enemy.
Sometimes you have to protect yourself from yourself.
Sometimes your own lack of judgment is your downfall.
And sometimes you need a little help to overcome your guilt.

The Tag-a-Long Ghost
My husband and I were in the Bethesda/Washington, DC area in 2008 to settle my mother-in-law's estate. We found this tedious work to be quite challenging, so after weeks of working on endless details, we decided to take a day off to visit some of the museums in the DC area. We took the train and greatly enjoyed the Arboretum and one of my favorites, the Smithsonian.

We also wandered some of the leafy tree-lined streets in the Bethesda area, enjoyed the quaint restaurants and strolled by a few of the charming hotels. My husband grew up in this town and he noted how interesting it was to see how an area changes.

Once we returned to the house Troy grew up in, we turned in for the night, but Troy kept having the feeling that there was someone else with us, someone else in the house. He kept seeing someone, a man, out of the corner of his eye. Troy was not used to seeing or sensing ghosts. He found it unnerving to feel this in the dark. I think men don't like feeling afraid or unable to deal with an unknown reality. He insisted that I take 'a look.' He asked me if I felt it. I think I was too exhausted to feel much of anything, but I agreed to look around.

Good Guy Bad Guy

I remote viewed my mother-in-law's house, top to bottom, all six floors of it. Finally, sitting on the old, worn, teal-colored carpeted stairs was a most forlorn ghost. He was dressed in a nice looking grey, pinstriped suit, but his suit jacket was askew, and his starched white shirt was no longer fully tucked into his blood-stained pants. His loosened, thin red and dark blue striped tie was no longer neatly arranged around his collar. His disheveled light brown hair looked as if he had spent many hours running his fingers through it in a worried frenzy. His once bright green eyes were dull with depression and the lines in his face told me he had seen far more than he had ever wanted to witness.

"Excuse me, who are you and what are you doing in this house? How'd you get in here?"

"I followed you home today. You looked like you could help me, and I followed your husband into the house.

The Witness Protection Program

"Do you know how many people walk the streets of this city? Thousands a day and none of them can see me. I guess I must've watched millions of people walk by since I died. When I saw you pass by, you didn't look like the other people. You looked different, shimmery sort of."

"Shimmery? Do you mean you could see my auric field or that sort of force field that extends out from a person's body?"

"Yeah, that, whatever you called it, it looked kinda' bright. I don't know what you mean by a 'force field,' never heard of that, but somethin' about you made me feel hopeful that you could see me, maybe. But when we got here, you walked right by me and didn't notice, so I had to make your husband feel creepy and then you noticed me. My name's Guy Pierce, CPA, or I was a CPA, I don't know what I am now."

Guy looked toward his feet, expecting to see them and he seemed to become more forlorn when he noted their absence, even more than when I first saw him.

"Well Mr. Pierce CPA, what happened to you? Do you have any idea when you died and how?"

"Yeah. God, I was dumb! Stupid, so incredibly stupid! I just wanted a drink. Is that so bad? Just one little 'ole drink to steady my nerves. . ."

His voice trailed off as he once again analyzed his fatal mistake. I had the impression that he had had this self-deprecating conversation with himself for decades.

"Looking at your clothes I get the impression you were going to some sort of meeting and then you just had to have a drink? Is that what caused your demise?"

"Is that what they call a hit? Demise? Demise – who says that? Anyway, I'm an accountant – or I was an accountant in 1968. I am/was the numbers guy for my company, and I hadn't been with them too long when I was given a 'new account' to manage. I didn't know. You've got to believe me; I had no idea who this account was for. All I knew was that I got this big account for some 'I'talian guy who was bringin' in really big bucks for a simple 'I'talian restaurant. And he kept on bringin' in this big money, hundreds of thousands of dollars, week after week and then the money would move out of the account the next week. I studied his overhead, his credits, debits, his depreciation, and there was no explanation for where all this money was comin' from and goin' to, so I started to question it and I asked my boss, one of the partners in the CPA firm. He tells me to just manage the books and don't ask too many questions. He tells me this is a big-time client, and we just do what he tells us.

"I knew this was money laundering. I learned about this in college before I graduated a couple of years ago. It was kind of a new way to steal money. I wanted to know where the money was coming from, but my boss says to me to shut up, do what I'm told, and I'll be making big bucks pretty soon too.

"I guess I got scared. My boss was eyein' me every day, makin' sure I was keepin' the 'I'talian guy real happy. I knew this was wrong. I knew it! I knew I could go to jail for this kind of stealing. I didn't even want to think about what the Feds would call this. But I didn't have to wait long.

The Witness Protection Program

"One day the Feds sat down with me at a coffee shop while I was tryin' to eat lunch. I almost wet my pants when I realized that two FBI agents were sitting across from me in the booth. At first, they didn't say anything after they showed me their badges. I wanted to throw up, run out of the café, but all I did was begin to sweat a whole lot and it wasn't hot in that place. Finally, one of the Feds says do I know this 'I'talian guy I'm running numbers for. I say yes, I do. They tell me that this guy is part of a racketeering scam and that they have been watchin' him for a while. They want to know if I've noticed any money laundering going on. I hesitated. 'Ah screw it' I said to myself. 'What's the use?' I sang like a canary – I think that's what they say in the movies. They had to stop me and set up what they called a rendezvous so I could tell them what I knew. They wanted me to turn 'state's evidence' and testify against the 'I'talian mafia guy. God, I didn't know he was mafia. I grew up in a small town in Pennsylvania and just got this job after college and what did I know about the mafia?"

He seemed to take a deep breath or wished he could do so and looked down in shame. I urged him to continue. He had to get his sorry tale out.

"The Feds said that if I turned 'state's evidence' that they wouldn't charge me with racketeering, but that I would be forced to join the 'witness protection program.' I never heard of that, but it means that I get a new identity. They said it was a new program they started to protect witnesses from the 'mob.' I was terrified! Terrified – day and night. The Feds never stopped watching me. I was supposed to get them copies of documents. I felt like a spy in some Cold

Ghost Stories from the Ghosts' Point of View

War movie, only I'm not the spy type. Day after day I managed to make copies, photograph the tracking of all of the money comin' in and goin' out. Day after day the money moved, 'til it amounted to millions and millions of dollars. I had never seen so much money on paper. The Feds were thrilled with what I gave them.

"Every time I had to meet with the 'I'talian guy, my contact from the Mob, he wasn't the big Mafioso, he was just a flunky messenger - that's what the Feds called him – I had to deal with this – I don't know what you call it – fear? Shit faced fear. So, I took a drink every single time before I met him. The Feds said I was doin' a great job and that I was the linchpin for their entire case. But the pressure was too much!

"Then one day my boss takes me aside all suspicious like and tells me to be sure and not tell anyone or I'll screw it up for the whole firm. Apparently, the big Mafioso 'I'talian guy was givin' the firm a kick back of hundreds of thousands of dollars. I didn't have those records, but the Feds told me that they would subpoena those records and get them, that I wasn't to worry about that.

"I'm pressured from my boss, the 'I'talian guy, the Feds and to make matters worse, my mother kept callin' me askin' me how come I wasn't datin' some pretty secretary in Washington! I had to take a drink to go to sleep and a drink to have the guts to go to work every single day. There was no let up from the pressure and the fear. Hell, terror, call it what it was. I kept askin' the Feds when this would be over but all they would say was that they were building the case. Then I noticed that they started to follow me. Finally,

The Witness Protection Program

one of them sat in that same café one day and said I had better lay off the booze or I could compromise the whole case.

"How could I function without the booze? I never stopped. Guess I got addicted. I knew I was becoming an alcoholic but at this point I figured I could stop later.

"Finally, the day came when they sat in that booth and told me that they finally had enough evidence to go to trial and that they were setting up my new identity. You'd think that would be enough to get me to stop drinkin', but it wasn't. I knew I still had to face the 'I'talian guy in court and survive the trial. They said that they would put me under 'protective custody' in a hotel near the Federal Court House, which they did. They did what they said. I had a Federal Agent assigned to me night and day. I was so nervous that I asked them for a drink before I was to testify but they said I had to be cold sober on the witness stand so I couldn't have any booze. They said we'd all go celebrate after the trial was over but that the trial could take weeks. Weeks! Weeks in that hotel with no alcohol! I couldn't face it. I know I'm weak.

"One of the days I was in the hotel with the agent, he had to leave the room for what he said would be just a few minutes to confer with the District Attorney on the case and he'd be back in less than an hour. That was my chance. Just as soon as he left, I slipped out down the back stairwell of the hotel and went into the bar for just a real quick drink. I was in a dark part of the bar nursing my whiskey when a man who looked like a gangster sat down next to me in the bar. He didn't look like one of the Feds. I guess the Mob had been watchin' the bar, waitin' for me to get this drink. I could feel his hot breath whispering in my ear, telling me that they knew I was the snitch, that I was an 'alkie' who couldn't resist a drink. They'd been waitin' for me since I got to the hotel.

"I knew as he was telling me this that this was it, that I was a dead man. He says in a heavy New Jersey accent that 'that 'I'talian guy don't like snitches.' Then he kisses my cheek – the Mob's 'kiss of death.' Then I feel this sharp pain in my side. I felt it a couple of times and then I was standing by the booth staring at this guy stabbing me. Then he folds my head and hands around my drink, and he slips away and out the bar.

"I watched as my blood collected in a sickening red pool under the table. It was a long time before anybody came to check on me. I guess they thought I had passed out with my drink. Then I watched as all hell broke loose. My Federal babysitter found me. He swore for a good hour after he identified my body.

"I'm so ashamed of myself. But how could I start over? How could I be cut off from my family, from what I knew, when I went into that witness protection program? How could I ever be sure that the Mob wouldn't find me?"

"Guy, are you saying that there is a part of you that did this, went down those hotel stairs to get that drink because there was a part of you that knew the mob would find you? Did you do this deliberately to get it over with so you wouldn't have to go into hiding for the rest of your life?"

"Maybe. Maybe that's true. Hell, I don't know. I'm dead and I still want a drink so bad I can taste it. I keep tryin' to attach myself to guys in bars who drink, whisperin' in their ear to drink more. Some do, some don't. Some are weak like me. Guess I didn't help anybody, except the Mob go free. I feel horrible all the time. I guess God is punishin' me for my weakness."

"Frankly, Guy, I think you're punishing yourself. God doesn't seem to have anything to do with this. Tell me why you wanted me to 'see' you? What would you like me to do for you?"

"I don't know. I guess I wanted someone to know that I'm sorry for being such a weak person, for screwing up the Government's case. I disappointed all kinds of people. I just want. . . I just want to stop being afraid of everything or being alone and feeling the constant torture of wanting that drink! I thought being dead would make it stop, but it never stops."

He doesn't cry, but his chronic ghostly depression is truly its own torment. I had an angel place a healing blanket around him. Sometimes, there are just no words for such a situation. He stood there and felt the blanket embrace him. Then he looked up at the angel with a completely bewildered expression on his face.

"Guy, it's alright to go with this angel. You're finally safe from the Mob now, from your alcohol enslavement and from your own profound fear. See if you can see someone you know coming for you in that welcoming light. Go on, it's okay."

His mom met him. He left quickly with his divine escort, and he never looked back.

Epilogue

Alcoholics, smokers, gamblers, drug, and other types of addicts do not lose their addiction in death.

Ghost Stories from the Ghosts' Point of View

They can attach themselves to, or hang around a living person with their same addiction because they still crave the energy that was that addiction. A living addict acts like a host for that toxic albeit addictive energy. It is almost like a form of possession. Each ghost constantly urges that person to drink alcohol, use drugs, smoke or more. The desire for the taste of the addiction is as much a torture in death as it was in life. Perhaps this is why when someone is drunk, they have no memory of their actions, or an addict will say that he or she 'wasn't themselves when something bad happens. The effort to help a soul in this situation is extremely powerful because they only lose that addiction when they are able to cross over into the Heaven World.

It is a spiritual law that you attract what you fear the most. Poor Guy was terrified that the Mob would eventually kill him; it was precisely what he feared the most. On a certain level he seemed relieved when he was dead, when it was finally over. Yet his guilt further enslaved him in the 4th dimension for 47 years.

It is another spiritual law that when you no longer need an experience, it stops happening. Guy must have finally decided that he was ready for help, and he found it. I think he realized that he was ready to cross over into the Heaven World.

He struck me as a man who was a victim of a terrible circumstance, which did not seem resolvable to him even after death took his physical life. I know that he will receive the help in the next dimension that he desperately needs in order to find peace.

Explaining the Physics of Metaphysics

The Light of Transition

Helping a soul to move into that Light of Transition means that you have helped that soul move into the Heaven World. Anyone can ask for angels to come and help a soul to move into this light and on into the Heaven World. Even those who have died can ask for this help. Millions of people automatically move into the light. Not everyone becomes a ghost. Perhaps those souls automatically saw and embraced this wonderful light and/or asked for angels to help them.

Frankly, it doesn't matter whether or not you believe in anything psychic or supernatural. These things have happened to me, to my family and my clients. Perhaps some of these things have happened to you. Possibly something you will read here will be of service to you. Perhaps you will be able to help a soul to cross over simply by requesting Angels of Transition and saying The Crossing Over Prayer to help the soul of the person or the animal. Sometimes, it's that simple.

Stacks of Time

When you remote view, when you see the past and sift through time, you encounter things called stacks of time. We've all heard ghost stories where the ghost is believed to be from the late 1700's – a much older period of time. Literally, that ghost is from that stack of time.

It was once believed that time was a straight line, and that the energy of time simply continued in that straight line. However, Albert Einstein noted that time does not always travel in a straight line; it can travel in curves and shapes. It can also exist in something called 'stacks.' A stack of time is simply an era in which time can still exist. Perhaps the easiest way to understand a stack of time is to consider that we think nothing of ghost stories that talk about a ghost from several hundred years ago haunting a location – in today's time. How can this soul exist in a past time and current time at the same time? That soul can exist in the past and influence the present, because that soul is stuck in a specific 'stack' of time and cannot leave that stack.

This stuck soul may not understand that he or she is dead. This soul may have remained at a location for a wide variety of reasons. This is especially true in times of war. Some souls are continually fighting the same battle over and over. For that warrior, time does not exist, only the current eternally repeating moment.

A stack of time can influence current time. A person from a three-hundred-year-old stack of time can influence present time because he or she keeps impacting the energy of the current stack of time. That's why you can see, feel, hear, and sense them. The flow of energy around the ghost will impact the energy of the present day, currently living people.

Mediums who can speak to ghosts can do far more to help them if they choose to do more than just talk to them. Remember, if the medium can see and speak to a ghost then that ghost has not crossed over into the Heaven World. Once any soul has crossed over into the Heaven World, they do not return to the mortal world as a ghost except for two reasons: one is that souls are allowed to attend their own funeral and the second reason is that the soul can assist the living through the dream state, but only for a very limited time.

The 4th Dimension

There are millions of people who are familiar with the words of the 23rd Psalm. This Psalm comes originally from the Hebrew Bible and was purportedly written by King David. Zabur is the equivalent to psalms in the Qur'an. Whether or not you believe in the psalms from the Hebrew bible from the Old Testament, the Qur'an or elements of Christianity, there are some very interesting concepts in this particular psalm.

"The Lord is my Shepard; I shall not want.

He maketh me to lie down in green pastures;

He leadeth me beside the still waters.

He restoreth my soul:

He leadeth me in the paths of righteousness for His name's sake.

Yea, though I walk through the valley of the shadow

of death,
  I will fear no evil: for thou art with me;
Thy rod and thy staff, they comfort me.
  Thou preparest a table before me in the presence of mine enemies;
  Thou annointest my head with oil; My cup runneth over.
  Surely goodness and mercy shall follow me all the days of my life, and I will dwell in the House of the Lord forever."

It is significant that people from very ancient times have had a concept of God and an afterlife. What is the 'valley of the shadow of death' if it is not a description of the 4th dimension? Why was this passage written, if not to advise us of what to do at the point of death? We are told not to fear the evil that lurks there and there is definitely evil that exists in this dimension. But evil can never attack any soul unless that soul has the karma for the experience, no matter what dimension that soul finds itself. Even if a soul has the karma to be in that dimension for any length of time, this passage reminds us that God is with us and that we need to remember our connection to the Divine as we pass through this dimensional doorway. We are also reminded that there are wonderful things that await us in the Heaven World once we are there - but we have to get there first. Even in the 4th dimension, we are not without free will. Free will is the option to ask for help from God as we pass through this 4th dimensional part of the initiation called death because He is with us.

  The reason that this is important is that many ghosts do recall seeing the Light of Transition waiting

My Own Spiritual Service

for them, but they do not always move toward it, for a variety of reasons including the issue of worthiness. Often very religious people, people who know the 23rd Psalm by heart, do not move toward that light because they do not feel worthy. It is always wise for all of us to remember how deeply we are loved by God and that He will always welcome us home, regardless of a particular faith – or lack of faith.

What is this 4th dimension? Ghosts that I have spoken to describe a dark world because that is what they are seeing all around them.

The 4th dimension is many things to many people. For some, it is simply a passageway through which they quickly pass to the Heaven World. For others, it is possibly a holding realm, where souls go who do not have a frequency or vibration high enough to readily enter the Heaven World. Those souls may languish in this nether world or dimension. These souls do not realize that they can ask for help. Every single soul has the opportunity to ask for help. Heaven can await us all if we believe in our own goodness enough, and if we can overcome the anger and frustrations that often carry over from mortal life.

The 4th dimension is a place of no time. Whatever a person died in is what they will be wearing for as long as they are in this dimension. They are frozen there. Usually, they can see people around them who perished with them, but they may not be able to see people of other time periods or people who died like they did. There are also beings/creatures in the 4th dimension that can torment those souls there to a greater or lesser degree again, depending on the frequency the soul takes with them at death.

Ghost Stories from the Ghosts' Point of View

These dark beings that torment some souls are called Lower Realm Intelligences. These are the little dark guys some people call devil-like beings. Some people think of them as little torturers because their job is to torment souls in the 4th dimension who carry any unworthiness, guilt, or shame. These emotional traits will always seek punishment: karmically, you get what you seek or feel that you deserve in this realm. God is always with us to help us overcome these creatures no matter who we are, what religion we believe in or how we died. We simply need to remember <u>to ask for help</u>.

My Own Spiritual Service

Lifelong Study

I have studied metaphysics all of my life. It has taken me years to graduate from simply seeing and sensing ghosts or something supernatural to actually being able to do something to help these lost souls. Through an odd set of circumstances, I learned how to help them to cross over into the Heaven World. Ghosts live in the 4th dimension or astral plain. This is the dimension of ghosts, of those scary things that you, a mortal person can see out of the corner of your eye, and that create goose bumps on your body. The part of you that can see them is your subconscious mind.

Animals can see ghosts too. One lady tells the story of watching, to her utter astonishment, her new kitten play with a ghost kitten. When the ghost kitten raced right through a wall, her kitten didn't realize that she was mortal, and the poor kitty almost knocked herself senseless when the wall didn't 'open up' for her!

Like many people, I discovered at an early age, that I had some degree of psychic ability. The key is what you want to do with that ability. In my case, I decided that I wanted to learn how to help ghosts. Consequently, over time I developed the unusual ability of actually seeing into that 4th dimension and helping those souls who are still there for whatever reason. We all have some level of psychic ability and with due diligence, anyone can work to develop this particular skill. Psychic ability isn't a gift, it's a responsibility you use to be of service to souls, both living and dead.

Even animals can have a tough time understanding that they have died. And this service can also include helping animals to cross over as well. Sometimes animals are so loved that their owners cannot release them and inadvertently 'hold' them in that dimension, precluding their transitioning to the Heaven World. Your pets cannot greet you when you die if you do not help them to cross over. All creatures, human and animal welcome the assistance of someone who will help them to cross over into the Light of Transition, and ultimately to the Heaven World.

The Defiant Spiritual Science Student

When I was a little girl, around age five or six, I was told that there was no such thing as ghosts. Ghosts were not real. People who said that they saw a ghost were ridiculed. People did not believe these witnesses to the paranormal, and often considered them to be odd or more bluntly: a little nuts.

When I was a young girl in 8th grade science class, I asked my science teacher to help me to understand why the principle of physics that states that energy is neither created nor destroyed, did not apply to ghosts. If that physics law was absolutely true, then why would we deny that there are ghosts?

My Own Spiritual Service

What happens to the energy inside a person's body at death? Where does this energy go and how does it magically reappear at birth? How does this work? Not only was my science teacher unable to answer this, but also priests and clergymen steered away from the concept of ghosts as if it were some deep secret, never to be discussed.

When I was a teenager, ghost stories were about criminals or tragic Southern Belles who haunted the living or vampires who sucked people's blood. No one believed these things because they were too fantastic to be real, but I knew that ghosts were and are real.

As a young wife in Charleston, SC we lived in a profoundly haunted house even though the house was only 18 months old when we bought it. How can a new house be haunted? It was haunted because of the previous people who had lived on that land. It is because of this particular haunted house that I embarked on the journey to understand ghosts and to take the fear out of dealing with them. They need help. We can help them.

Because of this process of seeking to understand and help ghosts, I gradually noticed that I could see them and hear them. That ability simply grew and grew. I also realized that to clear a location, I did not have to personally go to that site. Through the power of mind or remote viewing, I could connect to a location and identify what was happening there.

Very often you will see that the ghost refers to me as the 'Light Lady.' When you remote view a location, you are projecting a bright consciousness to another time, place, and dimension. You have to be bright enough to be seen by the ghosts there who may be in terrible darkness.

When the ghosts see me approach them, they see a woman who looks like she is glowing from the inside out. This seems like a unique 'light' to them, hence the term 'Light Lady.' It appears to them that I am meeting them on their terms in their world, in their time, rather than just trying to speak to them from this current time and place.

I have heard thousands of ghosts tell me their stories. Hopefully, by sharing their narratives, you will be able to have a greater insight and understanding regarding this spiritual realm. Perhaps this book will also help each reader understand what to do at the point of their own death and how to move toward that divine light.

There Is No Religion in the After Life

I have assisted thousands of souls to cross over. I have worked with ghosts of all religions, in addition to New Age individuals who profess no particular faith, and finally souls would have no spiritual basis whatsoever.

In every single case with every single ghostly soul, angels willingly helped them whether or not the individual believed in angels, God, heaven, or any other spiritual element.

And I call these amazing beings 'Angels' simply for lack of a better definition; they transcend any religious faith.

Someone in my position cannot judge the soul in front of him or her. Neither I, nor the angels that I call upon, question whether or not someone is baptized, ever went to church, or believed a certain way.

My Own Spiritual Service

In the 4th dimension, religion no longer matters.

Whether or not you went to any particular church doesn't matter.

What you thought you believed about any other religion is irrelevant. God's love is not conditional on what church someone attended.

God has no religious prejudice.

God loves all the mortal and ghostly souls in all existence equally.

What determines what happens to a soul at the point of death is stubbornly defined by three factors:

1. The soul's ability to love and be loved. A soul who feels unloved and who has a difficult time loving others may have a hard time accepting the Angels and Light of Transition when they come for them. Truly, if you don't feel loveable, why would you think that God would love you?

2. The soul's level of guilt will determine their worthiness to be in the Light of God's love. Many times, a person's religious belief system causes him or her to feel guilty. If you are told all of your life that you are 'born in sin and will die in sin' why would you feel worthy of God's love when you die? In addition, if a person feels like he did not lead a good life, that he was a bad person, this guilt can hold him indefinitely in the 4th dimension.

3. The soul's belief in the divine, in an afterlife. Souls who do not share some spiritual belief in an afterlife will be lost and astonished at discovering that they simply keep on being who they have always been – but now they are dead. Yet each person will still be helped without any spiritual prejudice if she asks for help. Souls still have free will in the 4th

dimension.

The divine light of Christ meets each soul – whether or not you believe in Christ. The loving, gentle energy of the Buddhist nature embraces everyone who crosses over whether you believe in Buddhism or not. The positive aspects of all religions are all there in spirit, but not the damming guilt, the controlling fear, and the crushing intimidation of mortal man's often heavily encumbered religious interpretation of God and heaven.

Helping souls is a privilege. Remembering that each soul is loved by God will help anyone who wishes to be of service to the dead do this type of job with that critical, absolutely essential degree of humility.

The real job of any psychic is not merely to speak to a ghost, but to also help that soul to cross over.

The stories you are about to read are all true however names, locations and minor details have been changed to afford the living families their privacy.

Prayers for Sending Ghosts to the Heaven World

The following prayers are excerpts from The Lightworker's Guide to Healing Grief© and The Crossing Over Prayer Book@ and are provided to help anyone with difficult death situations.

The Crossing Over Prayer

This prayer will assist any soul to cross into the Heaven World. Once a soul has made this glorious cross-over from this transitory world of darkness into the glorious light of God, the soul will be restored, physically, emotionally, mentally, and spiritually. This prayer will also work on ghosts whom you may not know. This prayer offers all souls the peace of release into the arms of God.

The Crossing Over Prayer

Dearest Lord above,
I humbly request that you take
any and all souls, who have found
my divine light of service, into
the Heaven World,
right now.

I ask that an angel wrap each
soul in a blanket of healing light,
right now.

I pray that every single soul will use the Light Bridge
provided by my angelic team to transition into the
Heaven World,
right now.

I send love and healing to all souls
no matter how they died, no matter
their level of guilt, without any judgment
or prejudice whatsoever,
right now.

May the light of your love, Father,
embrace and keep all of these souls
now and forever.
Amen.

A Prayer for Understanding

This prayer will assist you in seeking answers to the often, unfathomable question of why someone you loved has died. The more you say this prayer the more you open yourself to the insight that can come from God.

A Prayer for Understanding

Dearest Lord,
I most humbly pray that I may understand the loving ways of perfect order.

I pray that I may understand the cosmic view.

I pray that I may find meaning in my pain and hope in my yearning heart at the transition of my precious loved one [Name].

Please grant me strength and insight so that in my healing path, I may be of service to others.
Amen.

The Compassion Prayer for Suicide

This prayer offers assistance in healing and understanding. Suicide is so painful for family members left behind. There are endless unanswered questions. Often there is a subtle level of guilt that some friends and family members feel because they are convinced that there is something they could have said or done that would have prevented this event from happening.

However, sometimes, we cannot know the pain and sorrow, anger, and internal turmoil that a person was feeling as they left this world. Sometimes, we are not meant to know these things. Sometimes, all we are left with are the questions for which there is no resolution.

Sometimes, all that we can do is pray to God and ask for assistance in healing the soul who so suddenly left and for healing our own bewildered hearts.

Eventually, it is critical to understand that it is important to provide assistance to the soul so that he or she can find the Light of Transition, and the hope of healing.

This prayer can be read completely, or you can read only the sections that are healing for you in this particular moment.

The Compassion Prayer for Suicide

Heavenly Father,
my precious one has ended his (her) life.
Therefore, I most humbly ask
that your gentle Angels of Transition
guide my beloved one to the Heaven World
right now.

I request that forgiveness be given, Father,
for whatever events or circumstances
led to his (her) decision to leave mortal life.

I ask, Father, that you embrace my dearest one with the depth of your compassion.

I humbly request, Father, that you provide healing to fill the dark, angry, or profoundly sad places of his (her) very soul, with the powerful restoration of the Light of your Divine Love.

My heart is aching, Father, with deep despair.
I pray that you will help me to understand
His (her) death with your light of compassion and without judgment.

I humbly pray, Father, for love and healing
for my entire grieving family.
Please help us to understand and accept this heartbreaking moment and the days ahead, with your Divine Grace.
Thank you, Father, for loving [person's name].
Thank you, Father, for loving me.
Thank you, Father.
Amen.

The Healing Prayer for a Murdered Loved One

This prayer is a difficult one to read if you are facing the death of a murdered loved one. Families facing this type of grief often feel betrayed by God, by the concept that God would allow such a terrible thing to happen to someone they love so dearly. Anger at God is not unusual in these times. Families feel that they are also victims of such a tragic situation. Sometimes, individuals find that they disconnect from anything spiritual including the concept of prayer or of healing in this way.

And yet, there can be no healing without God, without reestablishing that divine connection. Sometimes in the darkness of grief and tragedy, this connection helps each of us to hold on and move through each challenging day of dealing with police, detectives, courts and the often, endless unanswered questions.

Assisting the soul to cross over is critical to the soul's ultimate healing. However, letting go of someone who died this way is profoundly difficult. It is normal to want to hold on to the soul. However, releasing the soul to the divine will ultimately help all parties to heal. Souls who are released to the Heaven World, find that the Divine can restore them.

If this entire prayer is simply too difficult to read all

Prayers for Sending Ghosts to the Heaven World

at once, then simply read the section that works at the time for you. Each stanza is designed to stand alone.

The Healing Prayer for a Murdered Loved One

Heavenly Father,
My precious [name of person]
has been violently taken from me!
Therefore, I most humbly ask
that your gentle Angels of Transition immediately
wrap my beloved
in a blanket of your healing light and then
guide my them to the Heaven World
right now.

I ask that they receive profound
healing on every level, for the fear, pain, and trauma
he (she) may have suffered as death came.

I pray that now and always,
you will embrace him (her) with the
restoring Light of your Divine Love.

I am heartbroken that I did not get to say goodbye.
Please, please tell him how much I love him now and forever.

He didn't deserve for this to happen.
Please tell him how much I will miss him,
and that I will pray for him every night.

Letting go is so hard. But I know I must do this. I want him to heal in every way.

Prayers for Sending Ghosts to the Heaven World

And I need to heal too. I am so angry!
I am so hurt that this could happen
to someone I love so much!

We are all suffering and do not know how to heal.
Please help us to cope with this unending pain, and
the anger in our hearts.

Please help us to find the strength to fill our hearts
with your Divine Grace,
a bit more as each day goes by.

Above all, please help us to face the difficult days
ahead without him.
Please fill us with the Light of your Divine

Grace, to help us to understand and cope with this
heartbreaking moment.

Thank You, Father,
Amen.

A Prayer for my Beloved Animal

We all love our pets and yet when their light leaves our lives, we are often embarrassed to admit how heartbroken we are. Sometimes, we are made to believe that we should somehow just quickly 'get over' the loss of this creature that graced our lives for such a long time.

Grieve your pet. Pray for your pet. Honor the love you shared.

Prayers for Sending Ghosts to the Heaven World

A Prayer for My Beloved Animal

Heavenly Father, I most humbly ask that you guide my sweet [name of animal] to the Heaven World **right now.**

I ask, Father, that you provide love and healing to my loyal companion, my most beloved creature, my precious [animal's name].

I ask, Father, that this valiant animal be embraced with the healing Light of Divine Love.

I send gratitude to you, Father, for the time I had with this wonderful gift you sent me, this sweet and loyal creature.

I pray that my beloved animal will know how much I love her (him) now and forever.

I miss my friend, Father.
Please help me to heal my own aching heart.
Thank you, Father.
Amen.

Ghost Stories from the Ghosts' Point of View

Glossary

Affirmation
An affirmation is a positive statement that we say to ourselves to reinforce our sense of self and to heal some part of us that has been wounded.

Aka Cords
Aka cords emanate out from your solar plexus—the area just below your breastbone. This is the place where the cord extends out and makes attachments to everyone you have ever met, to every place you have ever been, and to everything you have ever owned or touched. The longer you are attached or connected to something, someone, or someplace, the stronger your aka cord is. Your thoughts also flow along these fine, filament-like energetic cords. This is why when you are connected to someone and that person is thinking about you, you often sense it. This is also why if you have powerful cords attached in a strong love relationship, you often feel it immediately when the person dies. There are many ways to understand how these cords are eventually cut. The more profound the relationship, the thicker are the

aka cords of attachment.

Angels
Angels are divine beings from the Heaven World who work in the 4th and 5th dimensions to help mortal souls. Human beings are not and can never become angels. Any mortal person can call upon an angel for assistance.

Angels of Transition
These are specific angels who assist souls to cross over into the Heaven World. Anyone can request their assistance as well.

Appropriate Realm
This is a location that people who commit terrible acts of violence are sent. It is a realm within the Heaven World where the fractured soul can find guidance, soul healing, and methodology for balancing the karma of the violent life previously lived.

Archangel
These are a group of angels who oversee other angels. They are considered significantly more powerful than perhaps the lower ranking angels.

Astral Plane
This is the area of the 4th dimension, the land of no time, space or gravity, the dwelling place of ghosts and other lower realm beings.

Glossary

Aura, Auric Field

This is the protective bubble, force field, immune system that surrounds the human body. This 'field' can be enhanced or corrupted based on what is happening to a person. The aura can change colors depending on the person's emotional state or condition. Some psychics and psychic children can see auras.

Clearing Resins

Frankincense, Myrrh, Benzoin and Dragon's Blood are powerful resins from Sumatra and the Middle East. When burned on charcoal disks these resins will clear a tremendous amount of predecessor energy, lower realm intelligences and ghosts. Neither sage bundles nor any type of incense will do this, only these resins.

Dimensional Doorway

We live in the 3rd dimension, a dimension of time and space and gravity. However, in the 4th and 5th dimensions, time, space, and gravity do not exist. The ability for ghosts to move between dimensions is greatly facilitated by a doorway between each dimension as well as the assistance of angels who act as emissaries to facilitate the transition.

Divine

The divine is a connection to God and a location where God can be found. It is the powerful, positive energy of the Heaven World. We all access the divine when we pray, send love and healing, and assist ghosts to transition to the Heaven World.

Divine Beings
These are Intelligences who inhabit the Heaven World and who assist mortals in the 3rd, 4th, and 5th dimensions.

Emotional Haunting
The feeling that a ghost or a location is haunting you because of how you are reacting whenever you are there. This can also be an experience from a past life that haunts you, appearing in your dreams or causing you to focus on a particular subject matter throughout your life.

Ether
This is another term for the 4th dimension, where ghosts exist.

Frequency
Negative energy, guilt, grief, depression, drugs, alcohol, and toxic people lower frequency. Hope, love, healing, joy, and delight raise frequency. All positive efforts raise frequency. This concept of frequency or vibration at any given moment may determine your level of health.

Ghosts
These are mortal people who have died and who have not transitioned into the Heaven World. They are now souls inhabiting the 4th dimension.

Healing Blankets
A tool any mortal person can request to assist any ghost. These blankets are infused with the essence of the divine and help raise the frequency of any soul to facilitate transition into the Heaven World.

Heaven World
This is the 5th dimensional dwelling place of God, Jesus, angels, and Divine Intelligences. This is the location a person reaches when he or she crosses into the Heaven World. This location also includes various appropriate realms where even violent souls can receive healing for the extreme fractures in their soul that precipitate terrible violence. They also are provided ways to work through the karma of the life just lived.

Intelligences
These are spiritual beings who can inhabit the lower astral or the Heaven World.

Karma
This is the spiritual law that states that for every single action there is an equal and opposite reaction. What you do comes back to you.

Ley Lines
These are the electromagnetic grid lines that cover the entire planet. These lines are critical because they define the migration routes that animals and insects

use. All beings depend on these ley lines to help find their way on Earth. Ghosts are often found in greater quantities along the intersections of some of these types of lines.

Light Bridge

This is the term used to describe the divine pathway, which connects the 4th and 5th dimensions to the Heaven World.

Light of Christ Consciousness

This is 'an energy' of light, which any mortal person can request to help a situation, themselves or a ghost who is lost, alone and afraid. This light facilitates transition into the Heaven World and soul healing, regardless of any person's belief in Christ, their particular religion or lack of religious belief.

Light of Compassion

This is a divine light that has the potential to live in the hearts of mortal people as well as in the essence of angels, Divine Intelligences and God. These light spreads love and care, hope and the promise for redemption, forgiveness, and healing for all souls.

Light Lady

This term primarily refers to the author of this book. This is how ghosts generally refer to the author when they see her in their 4th dimensional realm. She appears especially 'bright' to them, literally full of light, hence the reference to 'light lady.'

Light of Transition

This is a unique form of light that comes to a soul who is ready to transition into the Heaven World. This light is the bridge between the 4th and the 5th dimensions. Additional terms meaning to cross over into the Heaven World include:

Appropriate realm
Heaven World
Light Bridge
Moving on,
Crossing over
Bridge to the light
Crossing into the light
Light of the divine
The other side

Light Work

This is spiritual work that helps others in a loving, gentle, nonjudgmental, and non-prejudicial manner, regardless of that person's religion or belief system.

Light Worker

This is a mortal person who seeks to assist the living and the dead in any karmically correct, spiritual manner possible.

Lower Astral

This is an aspect of the 4th dimension, which is the home of very dark intelligences, lower realm intelligences and spiritual vermin. Some people and religions refer to this as hell.

Lower Realm Intelligences
These are beings who are also referred to as little devils, torturers, dark guys who inhabit the lower astral. These creatures can bring great torment to some ghosts stuck in the 4th dimension. These beings can also torture living people during the sleep state.

Metaphysics
This is a two-part word: 'meta' meaning beyond or expanding upon, and 'physics' meaning the study of matter in space and time. Literally, metaphysics is the study of physics beyond what we currently think we know and understand.

Predecessor Energy
This is the energy of past people, structures and events that have existed on a particular piece of land or location. This energy can have a powerful effect on those currently living on that property even if the dwelling is brand new. The following types of energy will make any area especially toxic: violent weather, fire, murder, death by almost any method, war, prison/prison camps, meth labs, assault, abuse, bombing – literally any violent act will have an impact on the land or location. The energy lives in the wood, the minerals of the earth and in any structure(s) on that site.

Psychic
This is a person who has at least one of many spiritual abilities beyond what science can reasonably explain. This person may see and hear ghosts. He or she may see into the future, sense things by holding

on to an object or be able to 'know' things not routinely expected.

Psychic Protection

Psychic/spiritual protection can include performing spiritual practices including blessing and prayer and requesting Divine protection. A person can wear specific stones for protection such as black tourmaline, tiger eye, kyanite, howlite, quartz crystal (which is continually cleaned and cleared after each use) and other radionics devices (see above).

Psychometry

Psychometry is the psychic ability to sense the energetic information of a location or an object.

Radionic Devices

These are devices a person can wear which changes the frequency of their body and is reflected in their auric field, making it stronger. A Radionic device can be a stone, or series of stones, a platonic solid, such as an octahedron, or tetrahedron, sacred shape, such as the Fibonacci spiral, the cross or star.

Reincarnation

This is the concept that we live thousands of lives for experiences. We gain the required experiences, die by some method, get stuck in the 4th dimension, or cross into the light, review those life experiences, choose a set of parents and then we are reborn again. A person can reincarnate from the lower astral which explains the source of violent people.

Remote Viewing
This is the psychic ability of being able to physically be present in one location and project your consciousness to another location anywhere in the world, transcending time and space. Once in that location the remote viewer may be able to scan the energy of an area and determine what is happening in the present and/or what happened in the past.

Resonance
In metaphysical terms, the simplest explanation is that you attract who and what you are. You will attract experiences to you based on who and what situations you are in resonance with at any given time. You attract to yourself others who are like you: The Law of Resonance.

Sage
This fragrant herb is wonderful for ceremonies and sausage. However: sage will never remove a ghost, a Lower Realm Intelligence, clear a space or remove predecessor energy.

Shadow Lands
This is the 4th dimension, the place you may find yourself if you are knocked out of your body and end up in an unconscious state and cannot find your way back to your body.

Shaman
The Shaman for any tribe is the spiritual advisor

for the entire tribe. He or she may also be the Medicine Man or Woman, helping the tribe to heal physical and emotional wounds. The term Shaman is one of great respect. Usually, these men and women are very proud, peaceful, and wise.

Soul Frequency

Every soul has a specific frequency that defines him or her at death. The higher the frequency of the soul, the easier it will be for that soul to transition to the Heaven World. However, often the method of death or level of guilt and shame will cause a soul's frequency to be much lower inhibiting their transition to the Heaven World.

Spiritual Laws

This is the theme and variation of the energy of karma at work. Each law operates in every dimension. Examples:

For every action, there is an equal and opposite reaction.

You attract to yourself others who are like you: The Law of Resonance.

You attract what you fear the most.

Stacks of Time

All time exists at the same time in a specific stack of time. A 'stack' is a specific window or layer of time where something tremendous happened. The energy of that stack of time will keep vibrating out. To heal the current era of time, you often have to heal the past. When remote viewing a specific location, the psychic must sift through what are called stacks of time to find the specific stack of time that is currently influencing present events.

The 3rd Dimension

This is the dimension of mortal time and space and gravity. Mortal, living people reside in the 3rd dimension.

The 4th Dimension

This is the dimension of ghosts where time, space and gravity do not exist.

The 5th Dimension

This is the dimension of the Heaven World, God, Jesus, Angels, and Divine Intelligences. We cross into this dimension as we enter the Heaven World.

Thought Forms

All thoughts are 'things' and these things are forms of energy, even if you cannot see them with your physical eyes. Some thoughts are so powerful that they can physically manifest as semi-visible objects and, in some cases, can manifest as physically visible to anyone. You may see them as orbs, or they may seem to be ghosts, or scary apparitions. Psychics who are well schooled can see them in the 4th dimension. Who creates them? Sometimes white magicians create them, and they can look like shafts of bright light. But the more common type of thought form is the type that is created a black magician and can appear to be something terrifying, either in human or non-human animal-like from. Visualizing salt raining down upon them, readily removes them for they do not have strength in their shape but before you remove them, it can be unnerving the first few times you see them.

Vibration

Please see Frequency.

Wraiths

These are intelligences, energies, and manifestations from the lower realms, from hell. They are dark, evil and can be terrifying. They may appear in a room, a home, or on a piece of property. They are, however, quite fragile and sending them a prayer, or the Light of Christ Consciousness will almost immediately cause them to disappear.

Glossary

About the Author

Tina Erwin CDR USN (Ret) has studied metaphysics for many years, gaining insight into the interpersonal relationships at the heart of everyday living. Her writing comes from an intense desire to know and understand the unseen world of action and reaction combined with a sincere desire to share this understanding with other knowledge seekers. Her first book, **The Lightworker's Guide to Healing Grief** is a treatise on how to help yourself or someone else to heal grief. Her second book, **The Lightworker's Guide to Everyday Karma** is a lighthearted look at applying the principles of karmic law to everyday life.

Her next books: **Ghost Stories from the Ghost's Point of View Trilogy Volumes 1, 2 and 3** introduced to people what it is like to be dead, what it is like to discover that the life you thought you were going to have, is never going to happen. Literally you see the ghosts' point of view.

Her 6th book, **Karma and Frequency and her 7th book, Soul Evolution** further help to explain how karma works.

Finally, by popular request, she created the **Crossing Over Prayer Book, 88 Extraordinary prayers to help the living and the dead.**

Her lifelong studies into the deeper meaning of events and actions were further enhanced by the experiences of a dynamic 20-year career in the Navy, working for the U.S. Submarine Force, retiring at the Commander level. Commander Erwin found the Navy to be a tremendous schoolhouse in which to study all the facets of behavior, from the worst to the finest levels of humanity.

Be sure to check out Tina's websites and YouTube videos below:

You can learn more about her books, and her videos on her websites: www.TinaErwin.com
www.GhostHelpers.com
or connect with her at Tina@Tinaerwin.com or Contact@GhostHelpers.com.

www.ingramcontent.com/pod-product-compliance
Lightning Source LLC
LaVergne TN
LVHW041609070426
835507LV00008B/178